Tremont Street Subway
A Century of Public Service

by

Bradley H. Clarke and O. R. Cummings

Bulletin Number 22

Boston, Massachusetts
Boston Street Railway Association, Inc.
1997

Tremont Street Subway – A Century of Public Service
Copyright ©1997, Bradley H. Clarke

All rights reserved. No part of this book may be
used or reproduced without written permission
from the publisher, except in the case of brief
quotations used in reviews.

First Edition

Published by the

Boston Street Railway Association, Inc.
Post Office Box 181037
Boston, Massachusetts 02118-1037

Printed in the United States of America

Front Cover: Rush hour at Park Street Station never seems to change. From day one, the station has been a scene of constant activity. The motorman of the open car carefully scrutinizes the running boards for boarding passengers, just as the operator of the today's Type 7 car studies the mirrors to judge the boarding conditions at the doors before closing them. The ever-helpful inspector on the platform directs a lady passenger with child and dog to the proper car berth, and passengers are everywhere, waiting for the next car. *Courtesy of BankBoston Collection*

Rear Cover: At the outer end of the Beacon Street line, the first electric trolley line in Boston and Brookline, a watchful conductor boards a Victorian family, all properly dressed for the trip to town. After paying the conductor their nickel fares, they will enjoy a clean, fast trip downtown on an exclusive reservation for electric trolleys, and one that remains in use today for the same purpose. The Beacon Street line is the oldest operating electric trolley line in the United States, having been opened to the public on January 3, 1889. *Courtesy of BankBoston Collection*

Library of Congress Cataloging in Publication Data

Clarke, Bradley H.
　　Tremont street subway : a century of public service / by Bradley H. Clarke and O. R. Cummings. — 1st ed.
　　　　　p.　　　cm. — (Bulletin / Boston Street Railway Association ; no. 22)
　　　Includes bibliographical references (p.   ).
　　　ISBN 0-938315-04-8 (pbk.)

　　　1. Subways—Massachusetts—Boston—History. 2. Street-railroads—Massachusetts—Boston—History.   I. Cummings, O. R. (Osmond Richard). II. Title. III. Series: Bulletin (Boston Street Railway Association) ; no. 22.
HE4491.B8C58 1997　　　388.4'28'0974461—dc21　　　97-36385

Contents

Foreword 5

Before the Subway 7
    Alternatives to Horse Propulsion 9
    Petitions, Plans, and Legislation 11
    The Boston Transit Commission 13

The Tremont Street Subway 15
    The Subway Explosion 18
    Opening Day 19
    Rules and Regulations 21
    Opening of the Subway North of Park Street 23

The Social Significance of Boston's Subway 30

After the Subway Opened 35
    Elevated Trains in the Subway 35
    "Foreign" Cars 38
    Subway Modifications and Extensions 39
    Postwar Changes 46

Subway Rolling Stock 50

The Green Line Branches 53
    C-*Cleveland Circle*, The Beacon St. Line 53
    B-*Boston College*, The Commonwealth Ave. Line 58
    E-*Arborway*, The Arborway Line 60
    D-*Riverside*, The Riverside Line 62

Recommended Reading 64

The Victorians loved souvenirs. What better way could there be to commemorate America's first subway than with a view of the Public Garden Incline cast in the bowl of this very "Boston" spoon? *Photograph by J. David Bohl*

Crowds gather at the Public Garden Incline of the Tremont Street Subway on opening day, September 1, 1897. Note the signs on the dash of outbound No. 2580 and inbound No. 1795 advertising connections to cars serving the Norumbega Park resort in Auburndale which had opened the previous June 17. Open streetcars would be common sights in the subway for more than two decades. *Boston Transit Commission*

Foreword

THE TREMONT STREET SUBWAY, the first in the United States, opened modestly with little fanfare and no formal ceremony on September 1, 1897. It was a success from the start, carrying large crowds from opening day. The subway remains a success today, carrying more riders than any other Massachusetts Bay Transportation Authority (MBTA) rapid transit line as it has done for the last century. This book documents the developments which led to the subway legislation, the construction of the original subway, extensions to the subway, and the Green Line branches which connect with the subway today. While the concept of the subway took a while to evolve, the fact that it did so was no accident, for Boston had long been a leader in the public transit field.

Boston was the first city in America to build a subway, and the fourth in the world. The very first subway was the Metropolitan Railway in London, which opened on January 10, 1863. This was a conventional railroad, powered by coal-fired steam locomotives, with long underground segments. London's Underground was extended several times during the following decades. Dislike of smoky tunnels, however, precluded further subway construction elsewhere until new propulsion methods could be developed. The world's first electrically-powered subway, the City & South London Railway, opened in 1890. Unlike the multiple-unit electric subway trains which are common today, trains of passenger cars were pulled by a single electric locomotive. Trains operated in deep tunnels of narrow diameter, known as "tubes."

Electric propulsion was also used in Budapest's Földalatti (or "Underground") railway, which opened on May 2, 1896. The 2.3-mile-long line combined subway and surface operation in a private right-of-way. The electric cars were similar to streetcars, but regular city trams could not operate in the Földalatti because of low tunnel clearances. During the planning and construction of Boston's first subway, many comparisons were made with the line in the Hungarian capital.

The third city to build a subway was Glasgow, Scotland. The District Subway, or Central Railway, was a cable-powered line which operated in a loop around the city's downtown. It opened in the autumn of 1896.

The first use of electrically-powered multiple-unit trains in an underground tunnel was in the Paris Métropolitain (or "Métro"), which opened on July 19, 1900. This was the model for most subsequent subway construction throughout the world. Boston's adaptation of part of the Tremont Street Subway to multiple-unit rapid transit trains followed less than a year later.

Meanwhile, in New York City, there had been talk of building a rapid transit subway since the 1860s. At that time the city opted for elevated railways, largely because of the unsuitability of steam propulsion in urban tunnels. The subway debate began again in 1888, but no charter was issued until 1900. New York's Interborough Rapid Transit Company opened its first line on October 27, 1904. By the end of 1905, subway lines were also operating in Berlin and Philadelphia. There would be no further additions to the list of cities with underground railways until after World War I.

The Tremont Street Subway has achieved recognition for its premier status on several earlier occasions. In 1947, the Boston Elevated Railway (BERy) took note of the fiftieth anniversary of the opening of the subway in *Cooperation*, the El's employee magazine. There were also many articles about the subway in the Boston newspapers of the time.

On January 29, 1964, the U.S. National Park Service declared the Tremont Street Subway a National Historic Landmark. This event was commemorated in a ceremony, and by the unveiling of a small bronze plaque on the wall of the kiosk at the northwesterly entrance to Park Street Station.

The MBTA celebrated the 75th anniversary of the subway on September 1, 1972. The original commemorative bronze plaque (*opposite page*), located at the same northeasterly entrance to the south side of Park Street Station, was cleaned and repolished for this occasion. Speeches before a large group of guests and the public by MBTA officials were highlighted by comments from Edward Dana, former general manager of the Metropolitan Transit Authority (MTA). A trip to Quincy over the new South Shore branch of the Red Line followed, with a reception afterwards.

In a ceremony held on September 6, 1978, at the Boston Common entrance to Park Street Station, the American Society of Civil Engineers designated the MBTA's Tremont Street Subway a National Historic Civil Engineering Landmark. ASCE President William R. Gibbs cited the first subway in the United States as "a masterpiece of civil engineering and design." A bronze plaque was unveiled, attached to the subway entrance wall opposite the plaque erected on this kiosk in 1964.

After a century of use, the Tremont Street Subway retains many of its original characteristics. It has also changed in many ways, as this book will show. Apart from physical alterations, changes in name of various stations and the subway itself have been significant. Scollay Square Station was renamed Government Center in October 1963. This was followed in December 1964 with Mechanics Station becoming Prudential, in February 1965 with Massachusetts Station being renamed Auditorium, and in August 1965 with renaming of the entire Tremont and Boylston Street Subways and their branches as the Green Line. Years later, in March 1990, the name of Auditorium Station was changed again to Hynes Convention Center/ICA.

As this book is being written, the MBTA is promoting a year-long celebration of the Tremont Street Subway Centennial, featuring photographic displays, historic streetcars from different eras of the subway, and a planned public ceremony of commemoration intended to dovetail with the two-hundredth anniversary of USS *Constitution*.

The Subway was, first and foremost, conceived as a way to reduce traffic congestion. Speeding up public transportation was a secondary goal, but both objectives were accomplished. Within the first year of operation, the West End Street Railway saw seven percent of its entire revenue coming from just 1.8 miles of track in a system of more than 276 miles. This got the attention of the transit industry nationwide, and spurred the development of rapid transit in a number of other American cities.

Much of the information presented here comes from local newspaper accounts, records of the Boston Elevated and West End Street Railway companies, and several individuals whom we would particularly like to thank, including John V. Cahill, Jr., of Boston; Daniel R. Cohen of Boston; Kevin T. Farrell of Billerica; William J. Grimes of Watertown; George M. Sanborn, Transportation Librarian, State Transportation Library; and E. A. Silloway of Franklin. We would also like to credit the contributions of Richard L. Barber of Saunderstown, R.I., and the late Tolbert M. McKay of Londonderry, N.H.

Charles Bahne of Cambridge contributed an exceptional amount of background information for this book, including his insightful paper on the social significance of the subway, and his help was much appreciated. Stephen P. Carlson of Saugus provided many text enhancements, especially in the photo captions, in addition to producing a particularly creative layout for this book. Lorna Condon, Curator of Library and Archives, Society for the Preservation of New England Antiquities, made available a number of rare and unusual views from the SPNEA archives. J. David Bohl, Staff Photographer, Society for the Preservation of New England Antiquities, performed some demanding photographic work, including the photograph of the souvenir spoon and West End Street Railway badge shown elsewhere in this book.

Except as otherwise noted, all of the photographs in this book have come from the authors' collections. Most of the historic photographs in this volume were taken originally for either the Boston Transit Commission or the Boston Elevated Railway and its successors and are credited to those sources. Other images are credited to the photographer when known, not an easy task since railfans have always conducted a trade in pictures, often, unfortunately, not noting the original source.

The remarkable artwork on the front and rear covers of this publication was commissioned by the First National Bank of Boston in the 1940s for use on its calendars, and we deeply appreciate the assistance of Richard O. Card, Vice-President, Bank of Boston, now retired, and Patricia M. Donahue, Manager, Internal Communications, BankBoston, in making this material available for this book.

BRADLEY H. CLARKE
Boston, Massachusetts
O. R. CUMMINGS
Manchester, New Hampshire
August 21, 1997

The omnibus was the first dedicated urban transit vehicle. Although overshadowed by the horsecar, some survived into the electric trolley era as evidenced by this coach carrying the Boston Elevated Railway name. Following heavy snowfalls, omnibuses were often outfitted with runners and pulled like sleighs over the snow. This scene was taken about 1900 at the corner of Dartmouth and Boylston Sts. Due to bad weather, this omnibus is substituting for horsecars on the "Blue Line," which ran from Massachusetts Ave. and Marlborough St. to Scollay Square via Marlborough, Dartmouth, Boylston, and Tremont Sts. *Boston Transit Commission*

Before the Subway

THE EARLIEST PUBLIC TRANSPORTATION in Boston began in 1793, when a stagecoach line was started between Boston and Cambridge over the West Boston Bridge. During the next 50 years, stagecoach lines were established between Boston and many other New England cities. The stagecoach was better suited for longer journeys, however; by the mid-1820s a new form of urban transit vehicle had emerged—the omnibus.

An omnibus was longer than the stagecoach and could carry more people. It had lengthwise seats along the sides rather than cross seating between the sides, and a door on the back end rather than a door on each side. The most important difference, though, was that the omnibus followed local routes with frequent stops, unlike the stagecoach. Omnibuses began running between Cambridge and Boston in 1826. Service was hourly, and the line soon became known as "The Hourly." The fare was ten cents one way. The line was popular, and ridership grew so quickly that trips were increased to one every half-hour. Omnibus lines spread rapidly, and by 1849 there were 22 different routes in the Boston area, with fares ranging from five cents to a quarter. MBTA buses run over most of these routes today!

Horse-drawn mining railroads had been in use for some time, and it was clear that horses could haul passengers more smoothly and easily over rails laid in the streets than omnibuses could on the rough stone paving of the day, or worse, on dirt roads with ruts, which was more often the case. This led to the horsecar, which was first used in New York City in 1832. Horsecars took a while to catch on elsewhere, however. Boston's first horsecar line didn't start until March 26, 1856. It ran from Central Square, Cambridge, to Bowdoin Square, Boston, and, like the stagecoach of 1793, it used the West Boston Bridge. A second horsecar line followed on September 17, 1856, running from the old Boylston Market at the corner of Boylston and Washington Sts., Boston, to Eliot Square, Roxbury.

Horsecars were an instant success and by 1860 investors had organized 20 street railways in the Boston area. While some of these never materialized, by 1885, through mergers and leases, there were seven operating companies with nearly 232 miles of track, 1,716 cars, and no less than 8,374 horses! The largest system was that of the Metropolitan Railroad Company in Boston, Brookline, Chelsea, Dorchester, East Boston, Roxbury, and West Roxbury. The second largest, the Cambridge Railroad Company, operated in Arlington, Boston, Brighton, Cambridge, Somerville, and Watertown. The Lynn & Boston Railroad connected Boston and Lynn via Charlestown, Chelsea, Revere, and Saugus and also operated suburban lines from Lynn to Swampscott, Marblehead, and Peabody. The Middlesex Railroad Company served Charlestown, Everett, Malden, Medford, and Somerville, while the Highland Street Railway ran in Dorchester and Roxbury. The South Boston Railroad had six routes in Boston proper and South Boston, while the Charles River Street Railway ran mostly in Cambridge.

Travel on horse railways was slow, crowded, cold in winter, and hot in summer. Despite the lack of amenities, the cars made reliable and inexpensive transportation available to the average person. Horsecars were heated by small charcoal stoves, with straw sometimes scattered on the floor to help keep the passengers' feet warm. Destinations were usually lettered on the car bodies, and for illiterate riders, the cars were also painted specific colors keyed to routes and destinations. For example, yellow cars went to Jamaica Plain and

Cambridge Railroad horsecar 305 operates on the route between Harvard Square, Cambridge, and Bowdoin Square, Boston. Note the four-horse team, which was common in winter. This was the first horsecar line in Boston. *Clarke Collection*

Table 1

Street Railroads Serving Boston, 1885

Company	Track Miles	Cars	Horses
Cambridge RR	43.858	255	1,393
Charles River	12.187	58	377
Highland	19.116	187	977
Lynn & Boston	37.708	150	634
Metropolitan	85.038	721	3,502
Middlesex	20.704	152	639
South Boston	13.220	193	852
Totals	**231.831**	**1,716**	**8,374**

(The Highland and Middlesex companies were merged into the Boston Consolidated Street Railway on Aug. 21, 1886, and on Sept. 30 of that same year the Cambridge Railroad absorbed the Charles River Street Railway, reducing the number of operating companies to five.)

green ones to Brookline. There was a myriad of colors including carmine, blue, orange, and chartreuse.

Horsecars achieved an average speed of slightly more than six miles per hour. Despite this, ridership was in excess of 62 million annually by 1879. This was a 150 percent increase in a decade. The horsecar network continued to grow, but ridership grew even faster, topping 100 million riders annually by the late 1880s.

Horsecars were profitable, but were costly to run. However, from an operations point of view, they had many disadvantages, including the need for frequent changes of teams, especially in hilly sections and in bad weather; low operating speeds; requirements for extensive feed storage and stable facilities; the susceptibility of the horses to contagious disease; and the endless disposal of manure, a major problem.

While the horse railway companies served different communities around Boston, they all met in downtown Boston, sharing track in many places, and creating severe congestion when they came together. Consolidation of the separate companies was needed to allow cars to run through the center of the city from one outlying point to another, thus eliminating wasteful mileage duplication in the central business district. This is exactly what occurred in November 1887, when Henry M. Whitney, a Boston entrepreneur, brought the horsecar companies serving Boston, with the exception of the Lynn & Boston, into the giant consolidation known as the West End Street Railway Company. This was the largest public transportation system in the entire world at that time. Incorporated January 22, 1887, the West End absorbed the Boston Consolidated Street Railway, the Metropolitan Railroad, and the South Boston Railroad on November 12, and the Cambridge Railroad a week later.

Open horsecars operate past the Boston & Providence Railroad depot in Park Square in 1885. The B&P station opened in January 1875 and closed a little over 24 years later when B&P operations were transferred to the new South Union Station. *Clarke Collection*

(The Lynn & Boston Railroad grew steadily after 1887. By September 30, 1898, it operated a 125.76-mile trolley system, including leased lines and trackage rights, serving the cities and towns of Boston (Charlestown and East Boston), Chelsea, Revere, Saugus, Lynn, Swampscott, Marblehead, Salem, Beverly, Peabody, Danvers, Hamilton, Wenham, Everett, Malden, Melrose, Stoneham, and Woburn. After absorbing the Lowell, Lawrence & Haverhill Street Railway, the Lynn & Boston Railroad was renamed the Boston & Northern Street Railway on July 23, 1901. Nearly 10 years later, on July 1, 1911, the B&N absorbed the Old Colony Street Railway (operating to the south of Boston); and on August 5 of that year the consolidated property became the Bay State Street Railway. On June 1, 1919, the Bay State became the Eastern Massachusetts Street Railway, and on March 29, 1968, the company was

The last horsecars ran in Boston on Christmas Eve, 1900, on the Marlborough St. line. Car 562 seen here while serving that route had been built by the Metropolitan Railroad and was sold to the Central Park, North & East River Railroad of New York in 1909. *Boston Elevated Railway*

purchased by the MBTA and merged into the MBTA bus system.)

Government officials, legislators, business interests, and the riding public all realized that the speed and capacity restrictions and traffic congestion in downtown Boston were steadily limiting the ability of horsecars to do their job. It was generally agreed that the substitution of mechanical power for horses was a partial answer. Three distinct technologies to accomplish this were considered: steam railroad; cable, steam, and electric streetcars; and grade-separated, steam-propelled rapid transit.

Alternatives to Horse Propulsion

STEAM RAILROADS, which had led the way in the development of the suburbs, were faced with a steadily declining market share, a consequence of the more convenient and varied routes and lower fares offered by horsecars. Furthermore, there was no through railroad service across downtown Boston. Railroad commuter traffic was half that of horsecars in 1871, and had dropped to one-quarter that of the trolley lines in 1892. These disadvantages, in the face of declining public use of commuter railroads close to Boston, excluded conventional railroad technology from consideration as a solution to Boston's transit congestion.

Cable and steam-powered streetcars also received early attention. Cable cars were a proven alternative to the horse, having been operated successfully in San Francisco since 1870. The West End made an extensive study of a possible cable car line early in the winter of 1888 and found it only slightly attractive from an operating point of view. High construction costs ultimately made cable operation unattractive.

Cars propelled from power supplied by storage batteries also seemed feasible, and two vehicles were tested in 1887 with poor results. Another possibility was the steam dummy, a tiny steam locomotive concealed in a horsecar body, which could carry passengers and tow additional cars. Smoke, soot, noise, and premature track wear were the drawbacks to the steam dummy, and this approach was rejected as well.

The electric trolley was in its infancy in the 1880s; it would not be put to practical use until the end of the decade. Nevertheless, by 1885 the trolley car was thought to be promising. The West End Street Railway introduced the electric trolley car to Boston on January 3, 1889, when it opened to the public a new line from the Allston railroad depot to Park Square via Harvard Ave., Harvard St., Coolidge Corner, Beacon St., West Chester Park (now Massachusetts Ave.), Boylston St., and Charles St. An extension to this line to the Chestnut Hill Reservoir opened on January 12, 1889. Today's Beacon St. line from Cleveland Circle to St. Mary's St. is its successor, continuing over much of the same right-of-way. A second electric line was opened from Harvard Square, Cambridge, to Bowdoin Square, Boston, on February 16, 1889.

From then on, electrification of horsecar lines proceeded rapidly. In 1889, the West End had 7,728 horses, 1,794 horsecars, and 47 electric trolleys; but by 1895 there were only 857 horses and 541 horsecars, and the number of electric trolleys had increased to 1,714. In fact, by 1895, 94 percent of the entire surface track network of 296 miles had been electrified. It took until December 24, 1900, however, to eliminate the last horsecar line along Marlborough St. in Boston.

The trolley car was still subject to the street traffic delays despite its greater speed. In fact, the trolley's higher speed and capacity would be offset by further ridership growth. The use of trolleys quickly increased riding, in turn requiring more cars to handle the throngs of riders. The growth of trolley ridership mirrored that of the horsecar decades earlier and brought even greater problems. A photograph taken in 1893 shows a line of streetcars on Tremont St. between Scollay Square (now Government Center) and Boylston St. so tightly packed that one could literally walk along their roofs without interruption for several blocks. This severe congestion and the resulting public outcry forced the General Court (State Legislature) in 1891 to create a commission to study a comprehensive approach to public transit for Boston.

The growth of electric trolley lines in Boston was phe-

Early electric trolleys differed little from their horse-drawn predecessors. Indeed, many were converted from equine to electric motive power. Among the first West End Street Railway horsecars to be converted into electric trolleys was 1449, seen pulling a horsecar trailer in Harvard Square in 1889 on Boston's second trolley line. *Cummings Collection*

On April 14, 1897, a Lynn & Boston Railroad electric car heads down Cornhill St. from Scollay Square as it starts its journey toward Revere via Chelsea and Malden. The Lynn & Boston was the only street railway operating in Boston not to be absorbed into the West End Street Railway, and was the northern core of what would become the massive Bay State Street Railway system. *Boston Transit Commission*

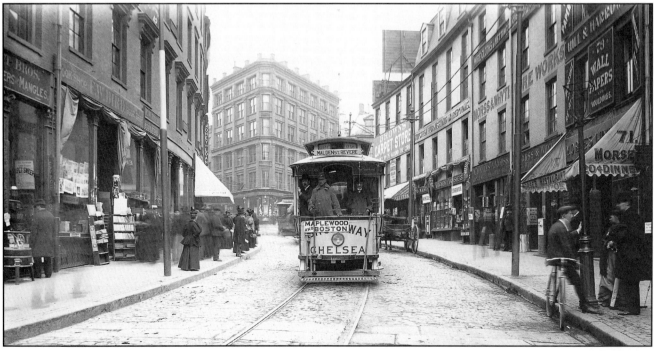

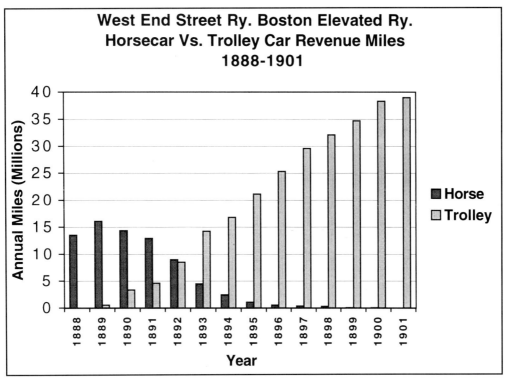

Figure 1

nomenal. In just a few years, most of the system had been electrified as shown in the accompanying Figure 1.

The most costly solution was rapid transit, a proven approach to handling high ridership levels. Rapid transit usually takes the form of elevated railways, subways, or surface private rights-of-way using multiple-unit, electrically-powered trains or streetcars. There are also other variations, which include monorails, buses on private rights-of-way, and electrified commuter railroads serving downtown areas. The first successful rapid transit system in the country was the Ninth Ave. Elevated of the New York Elevated Railroad Company. Motive power was originally cable; later, trains were hauled by small steam locomotives. Commercial operation by steam propulsion began on April 20, 1871, although demonstration trips with cable were run as early as 1868, one of them for a deputation from the Common Council of Boston.

Petitions, Plans, and Legislation

IN 1879, two groups of private investors proposed building elevated railway lines in Boston, citing the success of the elevated lines in New York City. The group led by L. A. Bigelow wanted to secure a charter as an investment. Charles E. Powers' group was primarily composed of established street and steam railway interests. The Powers group sought a charter as a hedge against the introduction of new transit technologies by other parties, which might pose a threat to their future business.

The Massachusetts General Court referred these proposals to its committee on street railways, which reported its findings in March 1879. The committee was unswayed by arguments about the safety and structural durability of the elevated lines in New York. Comparisons between Boston and New York were weakened by differences in street patterns between the two cities. The report also pointed out that neither group of petitioners was motivated by the need for improving public transportation. Finally, despite the Legislature's awareness of inadequacies in the surface horsecar network, there were very few written public complaints. In the absence of hard evidence, the lawmakers rejected both petitions. Still, something had to be done.

In March 1884 the State Legislature authorized the construction of an experimental steam-propelled monorail in East Cambridge. Named the Meigs Elevated Railway after its inventor, Joe V. Meigs, the line was an elevated monorail supported by single iron columns. The train consisted of a steam locomotive equipped with horizontally-opposed driving wheels and diagonally-opposed idler wheels, attached to a tender and a single passenger car. The entire train had a circular cross section, presenting a quite unconventional appearance. Despite its novel design, this unusual railway performed well under extensive testing.

In 1888 the General Court granted Meigs' company a charter to build an elevated railway line from Boston to Cambridge, but this was never exercised. In 1894, a legislative act to incorporate the Boston Elevated Railway specified the Meigs system for the motive power. This design never became a commercial reality: the original charter expired, and a combination of technological change and a lack of financing proved insurmountable, despite the 1894 legislation. By 1897, the defunct status of the Meigs system was formally acknowledged in new legislation which substituted electric for steam power on the Boston Elevated's first line from Charlestown to Roxbury.

In 1887 the West End proposed a downtown transit tunnel. Two years later, however, the company withdrew its plan after the benefits of consolidation and the technological superiority of the new Beacon St. electrification had become clear. Interestingly, this early tunnel proposal would be the plan that was eventually realized—it was the first glimpse of the Tremont Street Subway. The company later resisted petitions made to the General Court in 1889 from several parties seeking elevated railway charters, only to reverse itself in 1890 and make its own proposal for an elevated. This plan died, despite passage of an enabling act, due to public opposition which stemmed from the widespread fear of granting an all-powerful monopoly even more advantages. The public also suspected that the West End's proposal might be an attempt to block other interests from constructing elevated lines, and that the West End itself had no real intention of actually building an elevated railway.

Meanwhile, street congestion, primarily from growing numbers of trolleys and fewer and fewer horsecars, was steadily increasing. Despite many proposals for rapid transit, nothing tangible had emerged. The General Court finally decided to act, weary of public clamor for a remedy to the growing crisis, and spurred by an urgent appeal from Nathan Matthews, the newly-elected Mayor of Boston.

The Legislature had been inundated with many other transit schemes in the late 1880s and early 1890s, and it created the Rapid Transit Commission of 1891/1892 in response to this continuing pressure. Chapter 365, Acts of 1891, "A Commission to Promote Rapid Transit for the City of Boston and Its Suburbs," was signed on June 3 by the Governor. Appointments to the Commission were made by both the Governor of Massachusetts and the Mayor of Boston, as provided in the legislation. The Commission included Boston Mayor Nathan Matthews and City Engineer William Jackson, ex-officio. In addition, the Governor appointed John Quincy Adams, Chester W. Kingsley, and Osborne Howes, Jr. Appointed by the Mayor were Henry L. Higginson, James B. Richardson, and John E. Fitzgerald. The Commission was well into its work by late summer of 1891; on April 5, 1892, the commissioners submitted an extremely comprehensive report on improved public transportation for Boston.

The Commission recommended the consolidation of the then nine different railroad depots into two massive terminals, North and South Union Stations; many street widenings and rearrangement of street railway lines in these streets; and most important, proposals for a subway line and two elevated railway routes. The subway would run under Tremont St. and the Boston Common and would be used exclusively by surface streetcars. The elevated lines would run from South Boston to Charlestown, and from Roxbury to Cambridge. The two lines would roughly be in the shape of an "H," connecting at Causeway St., north of downtown, and again at Eliot St. on the south side. The downtown section of this elevated system would be diverted underground beneath the Boston Common and Tremont St.

The Rapid Transit Commission also pointed out that street railway ridership had doubled in each of the two previous decades. Mindful of this continued growth, and with the specific route recommendations in the report, the Legislature passed two bills in 1893. The first bill created a Metropolitan Transit Commission to oversee construction of an alleyway through the business district. The alley would have been parallel to, and between, Washington and Tremont Sts. The alley would be built at city expense, whereupon the Commis-

The experimental Meigs steam-powered elevated train is seen on its full-scale test track in East Cambridge in 1884. While the Meigs system initially was specified for Boston's elevated railway system, it was supplanted by cleaner and more practical electric propulsion. *Clarke Collection*

The streetcar congestion on Tremont Street is clearly evident in this August 1895 view taken from in front of the Park Street Church. A West End Street Railway survey the previous December showed that 215 northbound and 191 southbound trips per hour passed this point at peak periods. Note the one closed car on the Huntington Avenue service amid the sea of open trolleys. *Boston Transit Commission*

sion would auction the right to build and operate an elevated line through the alley. The Boston electorate defeated this plan in a referendum which was required because city funds were involved.

The General Court's second bill would succeed. Chapter 478, Acts of 1893, created, subject to approval of the Boston City Council, a three-man Board of Subway Commissioners appointed by the Mayor. The board was charged by the Legislature to report on the feasibility of building a subway under Boston Common to remove streetcar traffic from Tremont St. The City Council gave its consent for formation of the board, and the board members were appointed on January 1, 1894.

Subway routing, construction techniques, and cost were evaluated. The recommendations that emerged were so different from those envisaged by the General Court, however, that the Commission suggested amendments to the legislation that had created the Commission itself. The major reason for the proposed changes was that the Commission had estimated that the cost of the project would be at least $5,000,000, more than triple the original estimates. Providing an alternative method of financing the subway construction was needed. The lawmakers responded by appointing a Special Joint Committee on Transportation to review the subway project in greater detail.

The Boston Transit Commission

AFTER HEARING FROM CRITICS AND SUPPORTERS OF THE SUBWAY; various technical experts in the construction, transportation, and health fields; and from proponents of elevated railways who were led by the interested parties who supported Joe V. Meigs, previously mentioned, the General Court passed a bill on July 2, 1894, to create the Boston Transit Commission and the Boston Elevated Railway Company. The Transit Commission would be a governmental body whose primary function would be to construct the Tremont Street Subway, the proposed name for the new facility. The Boston Elevated Railway Company, on the other hand, would be privately owned, and charged with building elevated lines using the Meigs system; this section was termed the "Meigs Franchise." The legislation required a local referendum; Boston voters approved the bill on July 24, 1894.

The Boston Transit Commission was composed of the earlier Subway Commission, which included Charles H. Dalton, Thomas J. Gargan, and George F. Swain, plus two additional members appointed by Governor Frederic T. Greenhalge. The Governor appointed George G. Crocker and Albert C. Burrage on July 26, 1894. The Commission held its first meeting on August 15, 1894, and chose George G. Crocker as its chairman. On August 30, 1894, Howard A. Carson was appointed Chief Engineer for the Commission. The outstanding successes that this Commission would achieve in the coming years would result in its life and responsibilities being extended by subsequent legislation until 1918. At this time it would become the Boston Transit Department and continue until 1949, when it would be transferred to the new, publicly-owned, Metropolitan Transit Authority. Today, the traditional functions of the Boston Transit Commission are carried on by the Construction Directorate of the Massachusetts Bay Transportation Authority.

During the fall and winter of 1894-95, the engineering staff of the Boston Transit Commission took the Tremont Street Subway from the planning phase to final design. Groundbreaking took place on March 28, 1895, in the Public Garden. Construction went so rapidly that the first section was opened on September 1, 1897, from Park Street to a portal in the Public Garden, near Arlington and Boylston Sts. Two additional segments of subway were opened later. The leg under Tremont St. from Boylston Street Station to Pleasant St. (later known as Broadway) opened on September 30, 1897; and on September 3, 1898, operation began on the final section from the Haymarket portal to Park Street.

By 1903, after the temporary introduction of trains from the Main Line Elevated, more than 5,500 trips by surface and elevated cars were made in the subway each way each day. Park Street Station at that time ranked third among the railway stations in the world, in terms of daily riders, but had a comparatively small platform capacity of only 15,197 square feet. Despite this drawback, at that time more than 8,000 riders per hour transferred from surface to rapid transit cars at Park Street in peak travel hours. To handle these crowds, 250 surface cars per hour operated around the inner loop at Park Street, and 120 elevated cars per hour ran in each direction on the through tracks. All in all, the Park Street Station alone was handling more than 100,000 riders per day: the Tremont Street Subway was a phenomenal success!

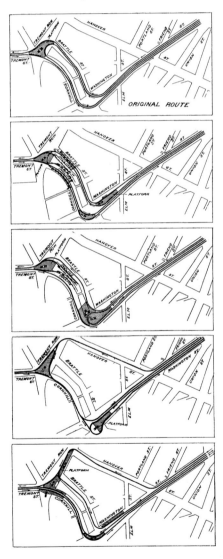
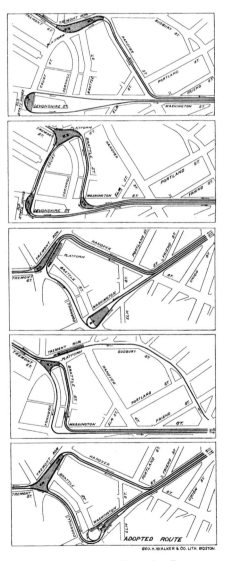

Although the legislation authorizing the subway described its general routing, the Boston Transit Commission spent considerable time determining the exact layout. This plate from one of its reports shows ten studies of alternatives for the line between Scollay and Haymarket Squares. *Boston Transit Commission*

The Tremont Street Subway

RANKING EQUALLY IN IMPORTANCE WITH THE ELECTRIFICATION OF THE WEST END STREET RAILWAY was the construction of the Tremont Street Subway by the Boston Transit Commission. First proposed in 1887 by the West End Street Railway and authorized by the State Legislature in 1894, it was primarily intended to relieve traffic congestion in the heart of the city of Boston rather than to provide rapid transit facilities.

Tremont and Washington Sts. were the two principal thoroughfares for streetcar traffic through downtown Boston. The former was particularly congested as many routes terminated along that street at various points between Boylston St. and Scollay Square. Indeed, an early photograph showed that at the height of the rush hour, one could walk on streetcar roofs for several blocks along Boston Common.

Construction of the subway began March 28, 1895, at the Public Garden, with Chairman George G. Crocker of the Transit Commission turning the first shovelful of earth in the presence of Governor Frederick T. Greenhalge and many distinguished guests. (Newspaper reports say that the governor just happened to be walking past at the time of the ceremony and was invited to take part in the program.)

For construction purposes, the subway was divided into 11 sections, each section being built by a separate contractor. (There was one case in which two sections were built by one contractor but the sections were not contiguous.)

As constructed, the main subway began at a portal near the intersection of Pleasant St. (later known as Broadway) with Shawmut Ave. and Tremont St., and it extended under Tremont St. all the way to Scollay Square The section between Boylston St. and Park St. ran under the easterly side of Boston Common. From Scollay Square, two northbound tracks ran under Cornhill to Washington St. and Adams Square and continued under Washington St. to Haymarket Square. Two southbound tracks ran under Hanover St. between Washington St. and Scollay Square.

At Haymarket Square, the ascent to the surface began, the tracks reaching ground level in the vicinity of Traverse St. and looping on a tract of land bounded by Haverhill, Canal, and Causeway Sts., opposite the present North Station.

Another section of the subway extended from the corner of Boylston and Tremont Sts., along the southerly side of Boston Common, paralleling Boylston St., and under Charles St. to an incline which reached the surface in the Public Garden approximately opposite Church St., now Hadassah Way.

The subway stations were Boylston Street, at Boylston and Tremont Sts.; Park Street, at Tremont and Park Sts.; Scollay Square; Adams Square (for northbound riders only); and Haymarket Square. There were four tracks between Boylston Street and Park Street stations. Turning loops were built at Park Street for cars entering from the Pleasant St. and Public Garden portals.

There were also four tracks between the Haymarket portal and a point in the subway beneath Hanover and Washington Sts. From here, two tracks ran under Hanover St. and Tremont Row to Scollay Square Station. One track continued south from Scollay Square to Park Street, sharing the tunnel with the northbound track to Scollay Square. The second track entered the Brattle Loop at Scollay Square Station, and was used to turn cars back from the north. It was in regular use until September 1952.

Leaving Scollay Square, the northbound track from Park Street Station and the track from the Brattle Loop both ran under Cornhill St. to Adams Square Station, beneath the intersection of Washington and Brattle Sts. These tracks then ran under Washington St., rejoining the southbound tracks under Washington and Hanover Sts. There was also a third track between Adams Square and the corner of Washington and Hanover Sts., which comprised part of a loop which had been built at Adams Square station. The Adams Square Loop appears to have been intended for cars of the Lynn & Boston Street Railway and was seldom if ever used in revenue service. On April 16, 1901, the loop track itself was removed in conjuction with track construction for the Main Line Elevated service. The third track leading to the loop was left in place until the early 1940s, and was used to for the temporary storage of disabled cars and maintenance-of-way equipment.

In all, the subway was 1.8 miles long and contained about

Construction of the Tremont Street Subway began with teams of surveyors laying out the route during 1895. This dapper rodman and an interested onlooker pose on the Tremont St. mall on Boston Common, in preparation for Boston's first "Big Dig." *Boston Transit Commission*

Subway Construction

Section 5

The southern end of the Tremont Street Subway was a four-track portal at Tremont St. and Pleasant St. (later Broadway). It would see surface trolleys from 1897 to 1901, elevated trains from 1901 to 1908, and surface streetcars again from 1908 to 1962, when it was finally abandoned. The tunnel which connects it to Boylston Street Station remains, and for many years transit planners have studied the possible reuse of this segment of the original subway. *Boston Transit Commission*

Section 1

Work on the section along the Boylston St. side of the Boston Common was complicated by the need to relocate bodies interred in the colonial burial ground, which can be seen at the far left in this October 7, 1895, view. Dr. Samuel A. Green, former Mayor of Boston and then Librarian of the Massachusetts Historical Society, was retained to report on a proper and respectful method of handling the remains. The Common burial ground was one of three cemetaries along the subway route, the others being the Granary and King's Chapel burying grounds. The Transit Commission placed a tablet to mark the site where the remains were removed. *Boston Transit Commission*

South of Park Street

Section 2

Framing for the subway had reached the point where the line curved off Boylston and into the site of Boylston Street station by April 7, 1896. This bird's eye view was taken from the Walker Building on Boylston St. Note the old Grand Lodge of Masons on the corner of Boylston and Tremont Sts. This building was replaced by the present Grand Lodge in 1899. *Boston Transit Commission*

Section 3

Section 3 of the subway extended under the Common mall from opposite West St. to Park St. and included Park Street Station. As can be seen in this June 2, 1896, view, much of the excavation was done by hand, with the spoil removed by horse and wagon. Note the trestle across the excavation which gave access to the rest of the Common from Tremont St. and the still-heavy streetcar traffic on Tremont St. to the right. *Courtesy of the Society for the Preservation of New England Antiquities*

five miles of track. On December 7, 1896, it was leased to the West End Street Railway for 20 years at an annual rate of 4.875 per cent of its cost, provided it did not exceed $7 million. (The actual cost was about $4.2 million.)

The subway was not built without opposition, for in those days, even as today, there were those stubbornly against progress or any change in the status quo. Some protested against the encroachments on Boston Common and the Public Garden; others feared the subway excavation would undermine the foundations of buildings along Tremont St., while others asserted that the removal of streetcar traffic from Tremont St. would prove ruinous to many merchants. Still others were opposed to subways per se and called for the construction of elevated roads instead.

Among the first obstacles faced was action initiated by the Merchants' Anti-Subway League which, in April 1894, presented a petition to the Massachusetts General Court praying that the subway should not be constructed but that elevated lines should be substituted. Partly as a result of this action, the Legislature ordered a city-wide referendum on the legislative act authorizing the subway. This was held July 24, 1894, and of the total of 29,695 voters, barely one-third of those eligible, who cast ballots, 15,483 favored the subway and 14,212 were opposed.

Even after the measure had won at the polls, opposition continued. On January 26, 1895, a bill to repeal the Subway Act of 1894 was submitted to the General Court. Given an adverse report by the Joint Committee on Metropolitan Affairs, it was rejected in the House. Court proceedings were then initiated. A bill in equity, seeking a temporary injunction against the Boston Transit Commission, was filed in Superior Court, which denied the motion. The complainants made some amendments to the bill and the respondent immediately filed a demurrer. The matter was brought before the State Supreme Judicial Court, and on June 15, 1896, the bill was dismissed. Pending the final court decision, work on the subway continued without delay.

The Subway Explosion

IN ADDITION TO THE LITIGATION, the construction of the subway was marked by tragedy. Shortly before noon on March 4, 1897, illuminating gas, leaking into an excavation between the top of the subway and a temporary bridge at Tremont and Boylston Sts., exploded. Six persons were killed instantly and four died later of injuries suffered in the blast; many others were hurt, some seriously. One four-wheel closed electric car of the Mt. Auburn line was demolished, a Back Bay closed horsecar was wrecked beyond repair, and a Brookline via Huntington Ave. eight-wheel closed car was badly damaged. Numerous plate glass windows in nearby buildings were blown out.

Commenting on the explosion, the *Standard*, an insurance publication, noted that the liability for the blast appeared to rest with the Boston Gas Light Company:

> The odor of gas was almost overpowering in the vicinity for a long time prior to the explosion and the company had been notified of the existence of a leak from at least two different sources during the forenoon, and the failure to remedy the trouble led to the fearful result.... Occurring as it did at a busy time of the day, it is surprising that more people were not killed outright.

Many suits were filed, of course, and the gas company had to pay heavy damages to the families of those killed or fatally injured in the explosion and to dozens of others who claimed injury as a result of the blast.

In this remarkable view taken by noted Boston photographer N. L. Stebbins looking up Tremont St. following the March 4, 1897, gas explosion at the corner of Boylston and Tremont Sts., Boston firemen continue to douse the flames amid a sea of wreckage of car 461. Horsecar 391 (center rear) was so badly damaged that it was scrapped, but 25-foot closed car 1113 (left rear) was repaired and returned to service. This was the single most costly accident which occurred during the construction of the subway. *Courtesy of the Society for the Preservation of New England Antiquities*

Opening Day

THE FIRST CONSTRUCTION CAR ENTERED THE SUBWAY on May 13, 1897, and nearly two months later, on July 3, a passenger car, carrying railway and state officials and invited guests, made an inspection trip from the Public Garden portal to Park Street Station and return. On August 30 and 31, the West End operated cars at frequent intervals through part of the subway to instruct motormen and conductors in the intricacies of the new facility, and on Wednesday, September 1, the section of the subway between the Public Garden portal and Park Street Station was opened to public travel.

Reporting on the opening of the subway, the *Boston Traveler* of September 1 said in part:

> At one minute before 6 o'clock this morning, the first regular car was run through the subway, and the event for which Bostonians have been waiting for two years and a half had come to pass.
>
> The first car through was 1752 of the Allston, Pearl St., Harvard Bridge line. It carried 145 passengers, among whom were two TRAVELER men.
>
> There was no formal opening. The car just came along and was switched in and went down the incline in the most commonplace, ordinary manner.
>
> The car bowled along, stopping at the regular stations, and dumped its load of passengers at the Park Street terminus.
>
> It was followed closely by another car of the same line and immediately after that came a Cypress St., Brookline, car. All were loaded to their fullest capacity with a gleeful, jolly, novelty-seeking crowd and everyone got the novelty.

The *Boston Evening Record* of September 1 noted that the crew of No. 1752 consisted of Motorman James Reed and Conductor Gilman Trufant. Supt. H. A. Pasho of Division 9 was on the front platform as the car entered the subway.

Describing the crowd aboard the first car, the *Record* said:

> The spaces between the seats were filled with standees; the platforms were packed like sardine boxes. Each running board was two deep with humanity, while both fenders were loaded down until there was not enough room for a fly to cling!

Conductor Trufant was assisted by Conductor D. R. Murray in collecting fares and they succeeded in registering 119—on a car with seats for 45 passengers.

The *Boston Daily Globe*, extra edition of Wednesday evening, September 1, 1897, carried the dramatic headlines: "FIRST CAR OFF THE EARTH. Allston Electric Goes Into the Subway on Schedule Time." This article said in part:

> Out of the sunlight of the morning into the white light of the subway rolled the first regular passenger-carrying car at 6.01. The car was from Allston, and it approached the immense yawn in the earth by the way of Pearl st, Cambridgeport, and the Harvard bridge. Conductor Gilman T. Trufant, an old timer in the employ of the West End, checked the fares, and motorman James Reed, whose hair has silvered in the company's employ, compelled the pent-up lightning to do his bidding.
>
> Over 100 persons were aboard the car when it rolled down the incline leading to the Boylston st maw, and they yelled themselves to the verge of apoplexy....
>
> Conch shell tints streaked the eastern sky when the earliest of those who made the trip put in an appearance at the Allston car sheds.... Birds were bubbling with the exuberance of morning, and the sun was kindling mock fires in east-facing windows when the motorman appeared with a six-inch to the weather smile dappling his countenance with happiness. Up over the car shed entrance a clock with gilded hands and sulphur-colored numerals marked 5.15. Thirty persons, two of them women, were then waiting for the start, and the majority of the 30 greeted the motorman. He was in new uniform, and he admitted that the anticipation of the run had robbed him of a great deal of sleep.
>
> Visions of the Cypress st car, spitting fire and hissing like escaping steam in its horrific rush to get to the subway

During the summer of 1897 the West End Street Railway operated special cars through the subway to familiarize motormen and conductors with the new facility. One of those specials, using 9-bench open No. 2544, poses for a photograph on the outer loop at Park Street Station. *West End Street Railway*

THE GLOBE EXTRA!
LATEST
FIRST CAR OFF THE EARTH.

Allston Electric Goes Into the Subway on Schedule Time.

THE CROWDED FIRST CAR AT THE SUBWAY ENTRANCE

Over 100 Persons Cheer for Allston, the Motorman, the Conductor and Themselves—Trufant and Reed, Faithful Employes, Had Charge of the Car—One-Third of the Early Passengers Were Women—Everybody Was Good-Natured, and the Historic Trip Was Pronounced a Great Success.

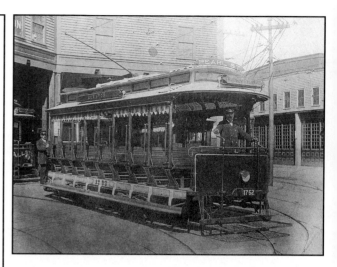

Open car No. 1752 was the first car to enter the subway on September 1, 1897. The *Boston Globe* article quoted in the text featured a drawing (left) of 1752 at the subway entrance. Shortly after the historic occasion, Motorman James Reed (Badge 9032) and Conductor Gilman T. Trufant (Badge 9019) posed with their car at the Allston Carhouse (above). Note the elaborate SUBWAY TO PARK ST. sign on the front of the roof. The 9-bench open had been constructed by the Massachusetts Car Co. of Ashburnham, Mass., in 1895, and survived until 1919. *Left, Boston Globe; above, Boston Elevated Railway*

first was his bete noir of the night, and he couldn't sleep.

"Every time I closed my eyes to whip around the curve into the land of Nod," he said, "I could see the motorman on that Cypress st car looking over his dashboard with flaming eyes and yelling, 'Another car behind,' to every one who tried to stop him.... Do you know, I believe that fellow is going to try to cut me off at the confluence of Huntington av and Boylston st, but if he does he will have to burn sand and manufacture pyrotechnics all the way in."

Others arrived while the motorman was talking, among them the conductor and a division superintendent of the road. The doors of the carshed were run back and Chief Inspector Fred Stearns very kindly reserved the front seat for the newspaper reporters. He made the trip on the footboard and frequently shouted cautions to the outside passengers to watch out for posts, trees and other things likely to raise bumps on any far outstretched heads.

Friends greeted the motorman and conductor once more as they took their positions, and after an inspection to see that the car was fit and ready, the current was cut in and the car run out to the street. More passengers had arrived, and the car, even before the starting time, was comfortably well filled....

All along the route crowds of men, women and boys were in waiting, and the air was peopled with uplifted hands. Another car was coming, but everybody wanted to be on the first one in, for all knew that, unless they were, they could not have anything worth boasting of. The seats were full, both platforms were crowded and the footboards were fringed, yet there always seemed to be room for one more. Boylston st was black with humanity when the junction with Huntington av was reached, and there was no Cypress st car in sight. As the run had been cleverly timed by conductor Trufant and motorman Reed, the passengers were not made uneasy by time-killing maneuvers.

Far down the street the entrance to the great tunnel was marked by a canal of humanity. The passengers aboard the car had packed themselves in like sardines, and the

On opening day, opens 3102, 2580, and 2392 meet at the Public Garden portal. The trees minimized the visual impact of the incline on the Public Garden. *Boston Transit Commission*

black mass, yelling like a jungle of wild animals, dipped down the incline for the underground run to Park st. . . .

Other cars followed quickly on the rear shunted cowcatcher of the first car, and at 6.30 the novelty of entering the subway was showing signs of age. It is a pleasant place, well-ventilated, well-lighted and good to look at.

Reports on the number of persons who rode through the subway on that first day of operation vary. The *Boston Globe* of September 2 gave an estimate of 200,000-250,000; the *Boston Journal* reported 75,000 and the *Boston Advertiser*, 60,000. All the newspapers termed the subway a success and clamored for its early completion.

The first lines to be routed into the subway were:

ALLSTON via Coolidge Corner
ALLSTON via Pearl St., Cambridge
ARLINGTON HEIGHTS via Cambridge
CYPRESS STREET, BROOKLINE, via Huntington Ave.
FIELD'S CORNER CROSSTOWN, for Ashmont and Milton
HARVARD SQUARE, CAMBRIDGE
JAMAICA PLAIN via Huntington Ave.
MEETING HOUSE HILL CROSSTOWN, for Dorchester.
NORTH CAMBRIDGE
OAK SQUARE, BRIGHTON, via Coolidge Corner
RESERVOIR via Beacon St.
UNION SQUARE AND SPRING HILL via Cambridge
WATERTOWN AND MT. AUBURN via Cambridge

These routes operated in the subway from 6 a.m. until midnight, running on the surface of Boylston and Tremont Sts. at other hours. Cars for Cambridge and points beyond, after leaving the Public Garden Incline, ran along Boylston St. and along Massachusetts Ave. to and across the Harvard Bridge.

Rules and Regulations

A FEW OF THE SUBWAY RULES effective September 1 are of interest:

At the foot of the entrance staircases (at the Boylston Street and Park Street Stations) are offices at which the admission of five cents must be paid, for which a subway check will be issued, which will be good only on cars taken in the subway and will be void if carried from the subway without using.

Holders of valid tickets and eight cent exchange checks can be admitted by showing same to the collector at the entrance office.

Eight cent exchange checks will be issued by conductors on receipt of subway check and three cents cash.

Subway checks cannot be purchased in advance for subsequent use.

During the debates over its construction, many people expressed concern over the quality of air and light in the subway. For the most part, they were pleasantly surprised. "The air is good, the temperature is comfortable, and the light-hued walls reflect the glow of many hundreds of incandescent lamps that brightly illuminate it," one commentator wrote. The last quality can be clearly seen in this view of open 2357 at Park Street Station taken on September 10, 1897, nine days after opening. *Boston Transit Commission*

Numerous surface car lines funneled into the subway. In late 1899 two electric indicator boards were installed at Park Street Station to show passengers the appropriate berth for the car to their respective destinations. Prior to these boards, riders were constantly milling about, looking for their cars. Afterwards, they only had to move when a definite berth for their car was indicated. *Boston Transit Commission*

On arrival at Park Street station, passengers who wish to remain on the cars for the return trip may do so upon payment of another fare.

To avoid accidents, persons carrying long or bulky articles, such as molding, pipes, etc., will not be permitted to enter the subway.

The admission of dogs is prohibited, also the sale of newspapers or other merchandise on cars, within the subway or on the station stairways.

The second section of the subway—from Boylston Street Station to the Pleasant St. portal—was opened on Thursday, September 30, 1897, the first car entering at 6 a.m. from Forest Hills, via Shawmut Ave. It was followed a few minutes later by a car on the Jamaica Plain via Tremont St. route.

Some cars continued to run on the surface of Tremont St. to a terminus at the Granary Burying Ground well into 1898. According to the *Boston Transcript* of October 7, these were as follows:

- GROVE HALL–COLUMBUS AVENUE cars which formerly went to Scollay Square.
- OAK SQUARE–BRIGHTON cars; a variable number during busiest parts of the day in addition to subway cars.
- BRIGHTON–NEWTON cars, via Commonwealth Ave.; variable number during the day to supplement subway cars.
- BROOKLINE–RESERVOIR cars, via Brookline Village; a variable number during the busiest parts of the day, supplementing subway cars.

As before, all night cars ran on the surface between midnight and 6 a.m.

Opening of the Subway North of Park Street

THE FIRST TRIP THROUGH THE ENTIRE SUBWAY—as far as Haymarket Square Station—was made on August 19, 1898, when a 9-bench open car, No. 2256, carried members of the Society for Promotion of Engineering Education on an inspection tour. Regular cars began running between Park Street and North Station via Scollay Square, Adams Square, and Haymarket Square on Saturday, September 3, 1898. A Grove Hall–Dorchester car, entering at Pleasant St., was the first to run through the entire subway from the south. A car on the Magoun Square–Roxbury Crossing route was the first car to run all the way through from the north.

Among lines diverted to the subway were the Grove Hall–Dorchester and Neponset–Union Station routes, both of which formerly ran on Washington St., and the West Somerville–Columbus Ave. and the Magoun Square–Roxbury Crossing routes.

In general, cars entering the subway at the Pleasant St. incline ran through to Union Station or farther north, while those entering the subway at the Public Garden portal looped at Park Street Station. Cars from Everett, Medford, and Malden via Charlestown, which formerly terminated on the surface at Scollay Square, used the subway loop there, as also did Lynn & Boston Railroad cars entering Boston via Chelsea and Charlestown.

Cars continuing to run on the surface (temporarily) after opening of the entire subway were those on the Forest Hills–Chelsea Ferry, Tremont St.–East Boston Ferry, Clarendon Hill–

All four tracks entering the Haymarket portal are occupied in this view taken shortly after the September 1898 opening of the northern leg of the subway. The two center tracks looped at Brattle St. (Scollay Square) and were used by cars of the Lynn & Boston Railroad as well as those of the Boston Elevated Railway. Note the close spacing of the two cars on the farthest right-hand track. Initially the subway had no signals, and operations were by line of sight, an unacceptable practice today. *Boston Transit Commission*

Subway Construction

Section 6

Section 6 of the subway extended from Park Street Station to Scollay Square. Staging for subway construction obscures King's Chapel on the right as a Back Bay horsecar and an electric trolley bound for Charlestown pass each other on Tremont St. on June 10, 1896. The King's Chapel Burial Ground was the location of one of the many ventilation chambers provided to introduce fresh air into the subway. *Boston Transit Commission*

Section 7

Contractors' sheds made Scollay Square a confusing place in August 1897 as trolleys, horse-drawn vehicles, and pedestrians all jostle for the remaining street space. The building with the awnings in the background is the famous Crawford House, while the sign on the second shed alerts people to changes in boarding locations for streetcars in the area. *Boston Transit Commission*

North of Park Street

Section 10

On February 8, 1897, the former Boston & Maine Railroad depot looms over Haymarket Square. Subway excavation is very much in evidence, and the station would soon be torn down to make way for the northerly incline from the subway to the surface. *Boston Transit Commission*

Section 10

The subway was built by the cut-and-cover method, whereby the area was first excavated from the surface. Concrete floors and walls were then constructed, followed by steel framing to support the roof deck. Once that was complete, the remaining excavation was filled and the street surface above restored. This April 1897 view looking south from Haymarket Square Station clearly shows the rough construction prior to beginning of finish work on the station and tunnel, which would take more than a year. *Boston Transit Commission*

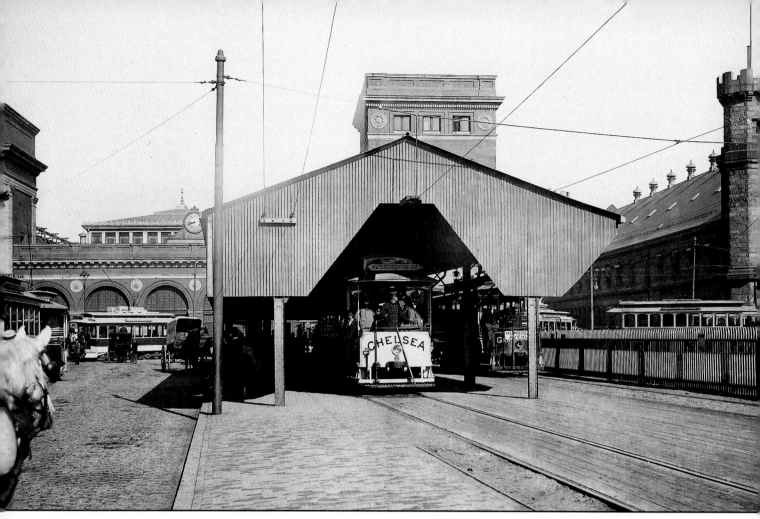

Lynn & Boston Railroad car 6 pokes its nose out of a temporary shelter over the waiting platform at Causeway St. on September 14, 1899. Note the numerous cars on Canal, Causeway, and Haverhill Sts., as well as both the North Union Station (left) and the old Fitchburg Depot (right), important destinations for Boston trolley riders. Construction of the Main Line Elevated would soon result in major changes to this terminal. *Boston Transit Commission*

Columbus Ave., Columbus Ave.–Union Station, Grove Hall–Spring Hill, and Union Square–Temple Place lines. The Tremont St. tracks also were used by Belt Line cars running north from Temple Place, Back Bay horsecars and evening trips from South Boston, Winter Hill, and Bunker Hill, as well as night cars.

Eventually, most of these lines were re-routed onto Washington St. Exceptions were the Back Bay horsecar lines, both of which were severely truncated. There were two routes, a "Blue Car" starting from Massachusetts Ave. and running along Marlborough St. and down Dartmouth St. to Boylston St.; and a "Green Car" running along Marlborough St. from Massachusetts Ave. to Arlington St., then through Arlington and Beacon Sts. to Charles St. Patrons transferring between horse and electric cars at Copley Square or Charles St. were obliged to use eight cent checks or pay two fares.

The legislative act of 1894 which authorized the Tremont Street Subway also required the Boston Transit Commission to order the surface tracks on Tremont and Boylston Sts. from Scollay Square to Park Square to be removed on or before the completion of the subway.

The Transit Commission voted on September 6, 1898, to order the West End Street Railway and the Boston Elevated Railway to remove the tracks. The work was begun October 1, 1898, and by the end of November it was complete. This move was bitterly opposed by certain merchants on Tremont St., but the legislation was explicit and the tracks came up.

An illustrated brochure, *Under the Hub*, published in 1899 by the Hotel & Railroad News Company of Boston, contained many items of interest about the Boston subway and some are deserving of quotation here:

STATIONS OF THE SUBWAY

THE BOYLSTON STREET STATION contains four tracks and two island platforms of artificial stone, and two stairways lead from the surface to each platform. The structure is of the steel and masonry combined type. The walls are lined with enameled brick. The westerly track (going southerly on Tremont St.) begins at the southerly end of the southbound platform to descend with an 8 per cent grade, passes by curve under the two Boylston Street tracks, and then begins to ascend at a 4½ per cent grade. There is a sub-passage six feet wide and about seven feet high, with a stairway at each end, connecting the northbound and southbound platforms.

THE AREA OF THE PARK STREET STATION is about one acre. Its shape and dimensions were limited by a law

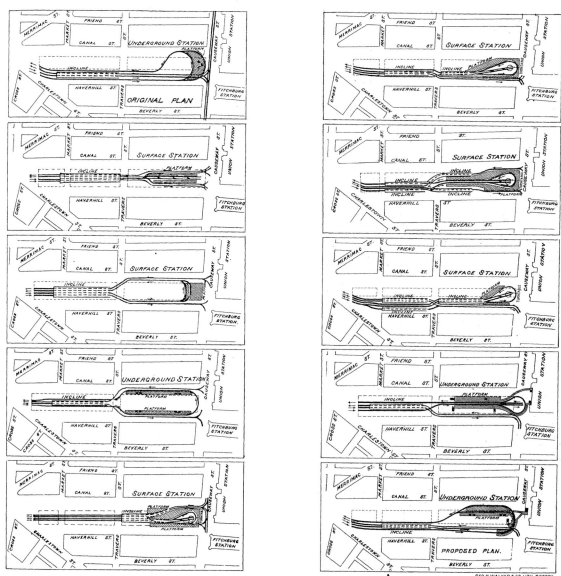

PLATE 1. SKETCHES INDICATING 10 STUDIES FOR CAUSEWAY STREET STATION AND CONNECTIONS.

Subway tracks shown thus ———————
Incline tracks shown thus - - - - - - - - - - - -
Surface tracks shown thus ———————

The arrangement of the terminal of the subway at Causeway St. was the subject of many design studies. Although the "Proposed Plan" (lower right) in this plate from a Boston Transit Commission report indicated an underground station, the surface station shown on the previous page was built instead. With interruptions for construction of the Main Line Elevated and its underground replacement, a surface station existed at this point until March 1997. At that time, the station closed as a preliminary to the construction of an underground replacement. *Boston Transit Commission*

passed to prevent undue encroachment on the Common, and in some degree by a desire so far as possible to save trees. The cost of its construction was about $350,000. The present traffic of the company indicates that during the first year of the use of the subway as a whole, the number of passengers taking and leaving the cars at this station will be at least as great as the number of passengers entering and leaving Boston by steam railroad trains at the Northern Union Station, or about 24 million, and also greater than the aggregate number of passengers last year entering the city by all the other steam roads which now occupy the new South Union Station.

IN SCOLLAY SQUARE there is one stairway for both entrance and exit, and one for exit only. Under the requirements of the Acts of 1897, Chapter 500, the Scollay Square station was enlarged from its original plan by the addition of a platform on the east side 198 feet long, with an entrance and an exit at the corner of Brattle St., for which the estate at this corner was taken. This addition gives increased accommodation for the convenience of passengers at this important station.

Suitable head-houses were erected over the subway stations at Adams, Scollay, and Haymarket Squares. Small

The *Boston Globe* of September 1, 1897, carried these two sketches showing the entrance to the southbound track at Park Street Station on the Common opposite West Street (left) and the ticket office at the northbound entrance to Boylston Street Station (below).

stone buildings were provided over the entrance and exit stairways at the Park Street and Boylston Street stations, four being constructed at each.

EQUIPMENT OF SUBWAY STATIONS

On the platform at the foot of the entrance stairways are the ticket offices, there being 27 in all. These offices are lighted with incandescent lights and heated by electric heaters. On the platforms at the foot of the exit stairways are turnstiles through which exit may be made; but which bar entrance to the platforms. Emergency rooms have been built in some of the stations, into which anyone taken ill or injured can be conveyed and remain until they can be removed. These rooms are equipped with a cot bed, chairs, table, etc., and are heated by electric heaters.

Each platform is connected by telephone with the company's telephone system, and, in addition, there is a system of telephones between stations so that the station masters can communicate with each other without calling up the central exchange.

MISCELLANEOUS DATA

LENGTH OF PORTION opened September 1, 1897, 2888 feet; opened September 30, 1897, 1,385 feet; opened September 3, 1898, 4,600 feet.

THE STATIONS ARE LIGHTED by arc lights; between stations, incandescent lamps are used. In the entire subway, there are about 4,800 incandescent lamps.

THE SUBWAY ON TREMONT STREET, south of Boylston Street and north of Park Street, is oval, or what is commonly called "barrel shaped."

A CAT BORN IN THE SUBWAY December 13, 1896, was named "Prince Subway" and was the first to ride through the tunnel, July 3, 1897.

FIVE MEN (four laborers and one carpenter) lost their lives in the work of construction of the subway; another laborer lost an eye. No loss of limb is known to have occurred.

TWELVE TOMBSTONES AND ONE HUMAN SKELETON were unearthed about 70 to 80 feet west of Tremont St., between the northerly line of Winter St. and Park St.

. . . In all, 910 bodies were dug up and reinterred in the course of making the subway excavations under the Boylston St. Mall. . . .

THE STATUE OF JOHN WINTHROP in Scollay Square, being over a part of the permanent work of the subway, was removed to a new permanent location, about 35 feet northeasterly from its original position. The statue of Samuel Adams in Adams Square was removed about five feet to the north and 2½ feet to the west, in order to make room for the side walls of the subway.

MOST OF THE SURPLUS EXCAVATED EARTH was loaded on Boston & Maine gravel cars and was hauled away at night, without charge to the Transit Commission. A smaller portion of the surplus earth was used to level up some low portions of the Public Garden and Common. A still smaller portion was filled on flats in Cambridge. The remainder was disposed of at various places, such as near the South Union Station, at Russia Wharf, etc.

The opening of the subway was among the subjects discussed in the 10th annual report of the West End Street Railway, dated November 10, 1897:

> The past fiscal year has been marked by two events in connection with the company of more importance than any that have preceded them—the leasing and opening of the subway and the leasing of the road to the Boston Elevated Railway. On December 15, 1896, a contract for

Grade separation in the Tremont Street Subway south of Boylston Street Station (drawing below) allowed South Boston and Roxbury cars to enter and leave the subway without delay. The Transit Commission referred to these tubes crossing one another as "bellmouths." This late 1897 view (left) looks south and shows the southbound Shawmut Ave. track running under the northbound Tremont St. track. *Both, Boston Transit Commission*

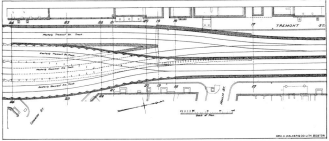

PLATE 26. PLAN OF SUBWAY NEAR COMMON STREET.

The subway stair coverings, or kiosks, were architecturally complex. Victorian ornamentation certainly was the order of the day as this view of Adams Square aptly demonstrates. This kiosk, designed by architect Charles Brigham, was a virtual duplicate of that at Scollay Square. Both stood in the middle of the street and featured clocks on the four sides of the central tower. Both were later replaced by simple, uncovered entrances. Compare this view taken at 10:48 a.m. on September 26, 1898, with that from February 1932 on page 44. *Boston Transit Commission*

Adams Square Station

Open 2107 waits at Adams Square Station for the Boston Transit Commission photographer to finish his work before proceeding to West Somerville. Adams Square served northbound cars only. The track at right leads to a loop—never used—believed to have been intended as a terminus for Lynn & Boston Railroad cars. Little patronized in later years, the station was closed in 1963 as part of the relocation of the northbound line between Scollay and Haymarket for Government Center construction. *Courtesy of the Society for the Preservation of New England Antiquities*

The Social Significance of Boston's Subway
by Charles Bahne

WHEN BOSTON OPENED ITS TREMONT STREET SUBWAY in 1897, the *New York Times* commented in astonishment: "That so conservative an American town should happen to be the pioneer in adopting this is viewed as remarkable."

Remarkable, yes; astonishing, no. Boston had long been a pioneer in adopting new forms of urban transit. And there were several reasons why a subway was considered the only reasonable way to solve the Hub's mounting traffic problems.

Until the 1880s, it must be recalled, there were only two practical methods of land transportation: animal power and steam engines. Both had major drawbacks as far as cities were concerned. Steam engines belched pollution even by 19th-century standards; their smoke, soot, cinders, and noise caused them to be severely restricted in some places. Horses were polluters too, and they were also expensive. They had to be fed each day, whether or not they were used. Only the wealthiest of urban families could own and maintain their own horse and carriage. Public transport—steam railroads, ferries, and horse-drawn street railways—was, for 95 percent of city dwellers, the only option besides walking.

Horse railways, developed in the 1850s and '60s, allowed cities to expand beyond a walking radius for the first time in history. Their effect on urban development has been well documented in Sam Bass Warner's study, *Streetcar Suburbs*. But by the 1880s equine power was no longer adequate. And horses, which could only work for a few hours each day, were a mounting expense for railway companies. One possible answer was the cable car, which allowed the energy of a steam engine to be transmitted under the street by a moving cable. Although cable cars are usually associated with San Francisco, over two dozen American cities had cable systems, including extensive networks in New York, Chicago, and Kansas City. They were considered in Boston, but the technology was ill-suited to its crooked and narrow streets.

The perfection of the electric streetcar in the late 1880s at last offered a feasible solution to the horse problem. Boston was the first major U.S. city to adopt electric propulsion on more than an experimental basis, in 1889. The speedy electrics allowed further development of more distant neighborhoods, such as West Roxbury, Hyde Park, and the outer reaches of Dorchester and Cambridge. Yet electrics brought their own problems. Residents of some fashionable streets refused to allow the erection of ugly overhead wires. In terms of keeping the neighborhood exclusive, it was a wise idea. Where electrics were permitted, they brought commercial strip development, attracted by the many riders who boarded and alighted at every corner. Good examples of this are Dorchester Ave. and Highland Ave. (Somerville); contrast them with Brattle St. (Cambridge) and Marlborough St., where electrics were excluded.

But the major trouble was congestion. Unhindered by other vehicles, electrics were speedier than anything else on the road. But they proliferated so quickly that downtown traffic soon became impassable. Boston's unusual topography, a remnant of the old Shawmut peninsula, only worsened the situation. Even the electrics found Beacon Hill too steep a climb, and no one dared suggest laying tracks across the Common! All cars from the rapidly growing western suburbs were thus forced south of the Common along Boylston St. At Tremont St. they met cars from the populous southern districts. Within the business district, only two streets—Tremont and Washington—were straight and wide enough for heavy volumes of streetcars. But even they were inadequate. In 1892, just three years after the electric car's advent, it was noted that "there is a space over a mile in length in the heart of the city where progress by car upon the surface can in no manner be made much faster than a foot-pace. Anything like rapid transit there is, in our opinion, absolutely out of the question, unless it be above or below the ground."

The sanctity of the Common eliminated many proposed solutions. Widening Tremont St. to 100 feet—including the demolition of the Park Street Church—was out of the question. A doctored photograph, depicting an elevated steam train chuffing past the church, was the death knell for that idea. So, by a referendum vote in July 1894, Bostonians decided that a subway was the answer. The Common would be violated, but only temporarily, and then restored to beauty (although many trees were lost permanently).

Underground still remained uncharted territory. Popular associations with the subterranean world were all unsavory. It was the realm of Lucifer himself, inhabited by lost souls, moldering corpses, strange forms of animal life, and noxious vapors. Reminders of the underworld were everywhere. At the Central Burying Ground on Boylston St., 910 of those moldering corpses had to be exhumed and reinterred. And when a workman's pick ruptured a water main, spraying the vilest of mud into the minister's study, the pastor of the Park Street Church denounced the subway as "an infernal hole" and "an un-Christian outrage." "And who," he asked from the pulpit, "is the Boss in charge of the work? It is the devil!"

Nor did it help that the station entrances, designed by city architect Edmund M. Wheelright, were decidedly tomblike in appearance. "They somewhat resemble the plainer type of mausoleums that are seen in the great cemeteries of Paris," sneered the *New York Sun*. "All they lack . . . is a carved name on the front and a few death's heads or griffins in granite to make them look a little more grim and gruesome." Whether as a result of this criticism or not, the later stations (Scollay, Adams, and Haymarket) were considerably more ornate, perhaps to a point of excess.

Another critic of the kiosks' architecture seemed to foresee the present day: "Such spaces for the talented bill-poster's work never were! Then, with the juvenile's taste for idle defacement, what is to hinder these blank walls from receiving their share of such attention?"

When the subway opened after all this, the reviews were nearly unanimous in their enthusiastic approval. True, the station interiors did not match the Doric-columned drawings published in the newspapers a few years earlier, but what did it matter? Those drawings were presumably forgotten, anyway. The subway was a "thoroughly agreeable surprise."

One writer commented on "that spacious archway with its solid masonry, its white walls gleaming brightly under its frequent jets of electric lights; its suggestions of largeness, of dignity." The same man raved about "the fine stairways, with their suggestions of solidity, of permanency; then, still further surprise, uniformed officers to look after the safety of the public; then, could I believe my eyes! placarded spaces for entrances to cars." Another spoke of the "massive tunnel, its forest of vertical columns, the grace and beauty of its outline, the effect of its thousands of electric lights upon the glossy-white interior finish, and the broad sweep of the smooth granolithic platforms." Only one critic lamented "the beautiful view of the Common in summer time which we all used to enjoy."

Questions of health remained, however, as the *Boston Post* of September 12, 1897, claimed that "Hideous Germs Lurk in the Underground Air." Next to that headline was a fearsome, 100,000-times enlarged sketch (below) of the "subway microbe" which occupied several columns across the newspaper page.

By 1916, the subway had become a necessary and accepted part of Boston life. When the Little Building, at the southwest corner of Boylston and Tremont, opened in that year, it featured a pedestrian tunnel directly into Boylston Street Station. Other tunnels connected the building's basement with three nearby theaters, so that patrons could walk from trolley car to orchestra seat without passing outdoors.

The Boston subway was the product of an era when public transport was not only public, but universal. Only the very wealthy could afford not to use it. Across the nation, virtually every city, town, and hamlet developed its own streetcar system. In crowded Boston, the subway increased traffic capacity by putting the trolleys underground, away from pedestrians and other vehicles. Boston soon expanded its subway system, and other cities such as New York, Philadelphia, and Chicago, followed suit. Today there are 18 different subway systems in 14 different metropolitan areas across the nation.

But our lives are different now. Automobiles—also an invention of the 1890s—have been mass-produced and mass-marketed for over 90 years. For most of us, public transportation is an option, not a necessity. The almost 700 cities and towns that once had streetcars have dwindled to just a handful today. Of these few survivors, however, nearly every one has a subway. And in the last decade and a half, more than a

THE SUBWAY MICROBE AS IT APPEARS UNDER A MAGNIFYING GLASS ENLARGED 100,000 DIAMETERS

The ultimate verdict rested with the riders, who thought it grand but who apparently still preferred to ride above ground. Commuters flocked to the subway, but casual patrons who rode "because it is pleasant" shunned it, "if for no other reason than because they won't walk down the stairs." Among this group were "the people who jump on a car and ride downtown, ostensibly to buy a spool of thread or a skein of silk or yarn, but really because the car is handy and the ride pleasant." Theatergoers seemed to avoid the subway, too, in spite of the fact that few Boston theater patrons were "of strictly carriage company." Some of this reluctance to use the subway may have been because the surface streetcar tracks on Tremont St. remained use for more than a year after the subway opened.

dozen new light rail systems have been built in North America. Several of these have included subways or similar tunnels.

Like the streetcars before them, autos have expanded our cities, enabling development of more and more remote areas. The downtowns of many cities have lost much of their importance, with acres of land devoted to highways and parking. Boston, on the other hand, remains the Hub of the Universe, a busy and congested place where half the workers still walk or take public transit to their jobs. The fact that we have remained a livable and viable city—and not just a collection of suburbs—is in large part due to the hole we started digging back in 1895.

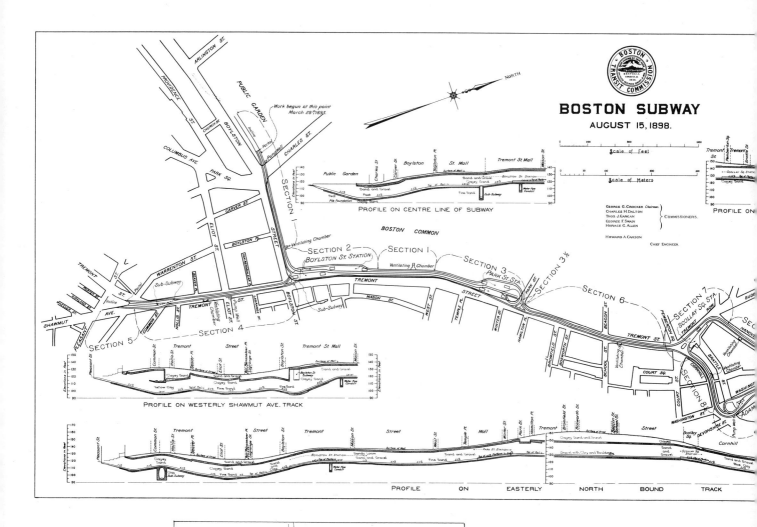

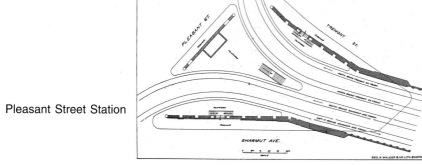

Pleasant Street Station

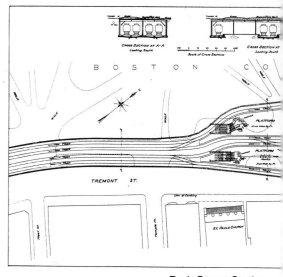

Park Street Station

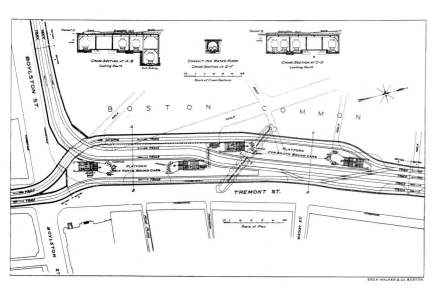

Boylston Street Station

TREMONT STREET SUBWAY, 1898

These plans taken from the annual reports of the Boston Transit Commission show the Tremont Street Subway and its stations as originally completed. The section numbers on the main map indicate how the work was broken down for construction contracting. In the century since the subway's opening, Adams Square Station has disappeared and all of the others except Boylston Street have undergone radical reconstruction.

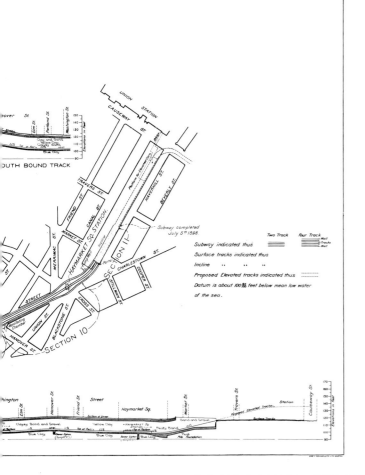

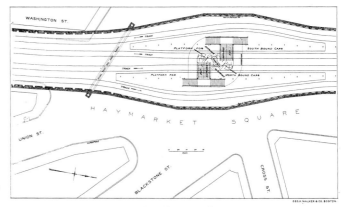

Haymarket Square Station

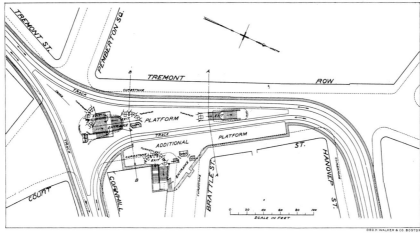

Scollay Square Station

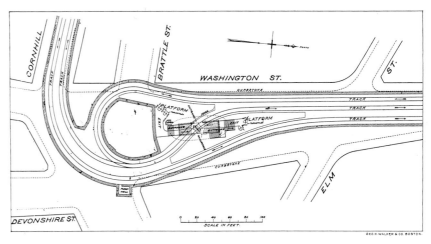

Adams Square Station

The Boston Transit Commission was justly proud of the traffic relief that the Tremont Street Subway brought to Tremont St. Contrast this shot taken on August 1, 1899, with the one on page 13 to see the difference. *Boston Transit Commission*

the lease of the subway, having been signed by the City of Boston and by the Transit Commission, and by your president, duly authorized by the board of directors, a special meeting of the stockholders was held and the contract was ratified by them. Subsequently, the contract was approved by the Board of Railroad Commissioners, and became binding upon your company for 20 years. . . .

The portions of the subway from the Public Garden and from Pleasant St. and Tremont St. to Park St. were completed during the past season. The completed portions are believed to be constructed in the most permanent and substantial manner.

The roadbed consists of an 85 lb. tee rail laid on chestnut ties bedded in a bottom of cracked stone about 14 inches in depth. On the entire length of this rail is a firmly attached guard rail, with a surface above the rail for travel of 7/8 inch, making a total weight of rail of 128 lbs. to the yard. This would seem to make derailment of a car improbable, if not well nigh impossible. No gas or oil is used in the subway. The lighting is from two entirely separate circuits, and the lighting of the cars from still another circuit, making the chances of the subway ever being in darkness very small. A complete system of hydrants connected with the city water has been introduced, with a full attachment of hose always ready for use if occasion should require. The same care and precaution has been taken in all the various details of equipment.

The portion of the subway in use at the present time is open for travel from 6 a.m. to 12 midnight during each day of the week. There are at present 1,362 trips per day being run through the subway. In the immediate future, three additional lines of cars will be added, making a total of 1,790 regular trips per day, with extra trips as the travel demands. This, in the busy hours of the day, when the largest number of cars per hour is being run, will give from two to three cars a minute leaving Park Street station, which is quite a tax upon the capacity of that station. Our returns show that nearly one-fifth of the passengers taking the cars in the subway during the day do so between the hours of 5 and 6 p.m. and that 90 per cent of these take cars at Park Street.

Our returns show that seven per cent of the total number of passengers carried over the entire system are carried through the subway.

The cost to the company of equipping the portion of the subway already in use has been large and when the remaining portion is completed, a large outlay for equipment will be required. The contract for the use of the subway and the cost of the cars of same, and the quite considerable force of men employed when the whole shall have been completed, will entail a large expense upon the company. . . . With only a portion of the subway open for travel, and that having been in use but a short time, it is too early to expect any judgment of the effect of the subway, when it is completed and in use, upon the travel of the road.

The opening of the subway has made it necessary to change the routes upon several of the lines of cars, it having been deemed desirable to have them terminate in the subway when it is practicable to do so.

After the Subway Opened

SUBWAY TRAVEL BENEFITED THE BOSTON ELEVATED and its patrons alike, for it consolidated loading points, simplified fare collection, and cut the number of stops. These led to faster operating speeds and lower power and maintenance requirements. In general the subway pleased everyone, including President William McKinley, who toured the tunnels on February 17, 1899. Newspaper accounts say that he and his entourage, which included Massachusetts Governor Roger Wolcott, were favorably impressed. When asked his opinion, the President replied, with considerable enthusiasm, "It's a grand thing."

On June 10, 1897, Chapter 500, Acts of 1897, was passed. This piece of legislative housekeeping amended the original Boston Elevated Railway Act of 1894 by substituting electricity for steam power for use on the elevated line (steam propulsion had been required in the Meigs Franchise), allowing the Boston Elevated to issue securities to raise capital, guaranteeing a five-cent fare, and establishing a legal relationship between the Boston Elevated and the Massachusetts Board of Railroad Commissioners. The way was now clear for the Charlestown–Roxbury elevated, which would open in 1901. The act also provided for a new transit tunnel under Boston Harbor to East Boston, and for two earlier projects authorized in 1894: a new bridge to Charlestown over which the elevated railway would run, and the Boston segment of a subway to Cambridge.

The General Court had granted the Boston Elevated Railway charter in 1894, but it was not until 1899 that construction actually began. The "Meigs" investors had been granted the Boston Elevated Railway franchise on July 24, 1894. Lack of financial support kept the franchise inactive, and the "Meigs" group attempted to sell the charter to the West End Street Railway Company, and to several other investor groups over the next year. The West End was content to stick to running its surface streetcar system, however, focusing its energy on the new Tremont Street Subway operation. The company also wanted to avoid the possibility of further public pressure in pursuing a controversial old idea.

A number of West End stockholders were dismayed by the company's inability to exploit what they regarded as a prime investment opportunity, and they joined a syndicate headed by J. Pierpont Morgan, the New York investment banker, to buy the Meigs Franchise. The purchase took place in December 1895, and the newly constituted Boston Elevated Railway Company held its first election of officers on April 10, 1896. The reorganized Boston Elevated Railway Company decided that the Charlestown–Roxbury elevated line would be unprofitable by itself and would have to be consolidated with the rest of Boston's transit network, i.e., the West End Street Railway Company. The fact that the elevated line would have to be depressed in the downtown area in the subway and that the West End was then slated to be the sole lessee of that subway was a major consideration. Finally, joining the two systems would ensure a single fare, a political necessity.

The West End Street Railway initially resisted the advances of the Boston Elevated. However, proponents of the lease successfully campaigned for proxies at the annual meeting of the West End, held on November 24, 1896. Their reward was the election of a number of new West End directors who were receptive to the idea of leasing the company to the Boston Elevated. The West End signed a 25-year lease with the Boston Elevated, the term running from October 1, 1897, to June 22, 1922. The Boston Elevated Railway now completely controlled the Tremont Street Subway.

Elevated Trains in the Subway

THE BOSTON ELEVATED BEGAN CONSTRUCTION of its long-awaited elevated line from Sullivan Square, Charlestown, to Dudley St., Roxbury, in March 1899. After somewhat more than two years of frenzied construction, the Main Line Elevated was opened on June 10, 1901, using the two outer tracks of the Tremont Street Subway from North Station to Pleasant St. through downtown Boston. Entering

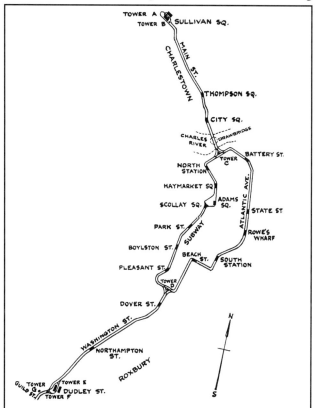

The original Main Line Elevated ran through downtown Boston by way of the Tremont Street Subway. *Boston Elevated Railway.*

Main Line Elevated in the Tremont Street Subway

A three-car Main Line Elevated train rumbles toward the Haymarket subway portal on June 17, 1901. From 1901 to 1908, elevated cars used the outer tracks of the Tremont Street Subway. Surface cars continued to use the center tracks. At this end of the subway, trolleys ran to Brattle Loop at Scollay Square Station. *Boston Elevated Railway*

To accommodate rapid transit trains, station platforms were raised, and this view of Park Street shows how it looked. The platform attendant's job was to slide open the center doors of the elevated cars by hand. Note the ancestor of the later day Information Booth to the right. *Rev. Michael J. Barry Collection, BSRA Library*

This artist's rendering, used on a 1905 Boston Elevated system guide, accurately depicts surface cars and elevated trains sharing Park Street Station. It is one of the best representations of the mixed modes which used this subway from 1901 to 1908. *Boston Elevated Railway*

Shots of elevated trains in the Tremont Street Subway stations are rare. This 1905 view is in Scollay Square Station in the northbound direction. Note the indicator sign to the left of top center showing the train destination. *Boston Elevated Railway*

At the south end of the Tremont Street Subway, elevated trains left the Pleasant Street Station and climbed a long ramp, as this train is doing, and then a bridge over the Boston & Albany and New Haven Railroads on their way to the Washington Street elevated structure. When surface cars resumed operation through this end of the subway in 1908, the ramp remained intact and was used in later years to store work equipment. *Clarke Collection*

at North Station, elevated trains ran through Haymarket, Scollay, Park, and Boylston stations on the outside rail (Adams Station, too, in the northbound direction) and exited at Pleasant and Tremont Sts. into a new station called Pleasant Street (Pleasant St. itself was later named Broadway). From here the trains returned to the Washington St. elevated structure on a ramp to a bridge over the New Haven and Boston & Albany Railroads, and part of Castle St. On August 22, 1901, service started on the Atlantic Avenue Elevated, connecting with the Sullivan–Dudley line in the north at North Washington and Causeway Sts., and in the south at Washington and Castle Sts. Shop facilities were built at Sullivan Square, and at Guild St. in Roxbury, just beyond the Dudley terminal.

Modifying the Tremont Street Subway for rapid transit trains was a tricky business. The Main Line Elevated was connected with the outer tracks of the northern end of the subway with specially constructed steel ramps which joined the structure on Causeway St. On the Pleasant St. end of the subway, Pleasant Street Station was built along with the ramp to a new section of elevated structure on Castle St., which joined the Main Line Elevated at Castle Square. Surface tracks were disconnected at both the Haymarket and Pleasant St. portals, and rapid transit tracks installed. Third rail installation was required between the Pleasant St. and Haymarket portals, along with an automatic block signal system. Raised wooden platforms were required at all stations to match the floor height of the elevated cars, and fare collection facilities were also altered. Sliding platforms were needed in addition in a number of places to fill gaps between the elevated car doors and the wooden platform. Because clearances were tight virtually everywhere along the route, the subway walls were cut away at many points to handle the larger cars.

It was evident from the start that the rapid transit operation in the subway would be troublesome. Typical problems included the wooden high-level platforms, which reduced pedestrian mobility in the stations and caused many step and tripping accidents. In addition, the tight clearances, sharp curves, and steep grades in the subway were all harsh on rapid transit cars running in a facility which had really been built for generally smaller surface streetcars.

The effect on subway-surface trolley operations was quite serious, because between Park Street and Scollay Square, there was no through streetcar service. All passengers between these points had to transfer to rapid transit trains, resulting in considerable rider inconvenience. Furthermore, the Pleasant St. portal was completely closed to surface car traffic. These drawbacks were widely recognized, and plans were soon made to build a new subway under Washington St. for the Main Line Elevated. This facility, the Washington Street Tunnel, was opened on November 30, 1908. Removal of high-platform and third-rail equipment from the Tremont Street Subway began at once, and on December 4, 1908, streetcar service was restored through all parts of the subway formerly used by the elevated trains.

"Foreign" Cars

THE BOSTON ELEVATED often permitted streetcars of other companies to use its tracks for occasional excursions from cites and towns outside its operating area. The company termed these visitors "foreign" cars. Sometimes as well, the Boston El would run its own surface cars far afield on similar jaunts. Gen. William A. Bancroft, president of the Boston El, often took long trips through the countryside in his private parlor car, No. 101. More important than these excursions, though, were regularly operated services by cars of other companies which ran into the Tremont Street Subway and other Boston Elevated facilities. The Tremont Street Subway operations will be covered here, including the operations of the Lynn & Boston Street Railway from the north to Brattle Street Loop, and the Middlesex & Boston Street Railway lines from the west to Park Street Station.

The Lynn & Boston Street Railroad (L&B) and the West End Street Railway had both applied to the Boston Transit Commission for the right to operate into the Tremont Street Subway on June 19, 1896. Both applications were approved. After the subway north of Park Street opened in 1898, the L&B—along with its successors, the Boston & Northern, the Bay State, and the Eastern Massachusetts Street Railways—ran through this section for nearly 37 years thereafter.

The Bay State timetable of July 8, 1912, contained schedules for nine major routes originating at Brattle Street loop in Scollay Square station. The longest of these, 17.21 miles, extended to the Beverly transfer station via West Lynn, Lynn, and Salem, while the second longest, 12.43 miles, was that to Swampscott via Central Square, Lynn. Others ran to Melrose Highlands via Malden, 9 miles; to Saugus Center via Linden and Cliftondale, 9.65 miles; to Beachmont (Revere), 6.75 miles; to Revere Beach via Beach St., 6 miles; to Revere Beach via Revere St., also 6 miles; to Washington Ave., Chelsea, 4 miles, and to Woodlawn Cemetery, 5 miles. Cars on all routes ran over Boston Elevated surface trackage between the North Station portal of the subway and the intersection of Chelsea and Vine Sts. in Charlestown, and crossed three drawbridges, the frequent openings of which played havoc with trolley service. The drawbridges included the Chelsea Bridge over Mystic River with its two draw spans, and the Warren Bridge, with the Charlestown Bridge as an alternative to the latter.

After the Bay State was succeeded by the Eastern Massachusetts Street Railway in 1919, there were no immediate changes in the routes operated from Scollay Square station. By November 1934 only seven remained. These extended from Boston to Beachmont; from Boston to Central Square, Lynn; from Boston to Town House Square, Salem; from Boston to Malden; from Boston to Revere Beach via Beach St.; from Boston to Revere Beach via Revere St.; and from Boston to Woodlawn Cemetery.

Because of the temporary closing of the Chelsea Bridge (between Chelsea and Charlestown) to all traffic, the Eastern Massachusetts discontinued trolley service between Chelsea Square and Scollay Square on January 13, 1935, and on the following day the company began running buses between Chelsea Square and Haymarket Square, Boston, via the new Sumner Tunnel. Cars to and from Lynn, Salem, Malden, Revere Beach, and Woodlawn connected with the motor coaches in Chelsea Square until June 10, 1936, when the Eastern Mass. sold its Chelsea Division to the Boston Elevated Railway for $1.5 million.

The Tremont Street Subway was still under construction on June 17, 1897, when Norumbega Park, a summer pleasure resort, was opened on the north side of Commonwealth Ave., next to the Charles River, in the Auburndale area of Newton. Served by the Commonwealth Avenue Street Railway, it immediately became a highly popular seasonal attraction, and the public began clamoring for the operation of through cars between Park Street Station and Norumbega, about 10½ miles.

Both the Boston Elevated and the Commonwealth Av-

An Eastern Mass. Street Railway 7000-series lightweight car rumbles down Causeway St. on its way from the Brattle Street Loop in the subway to Central Square, Lynn, in August 1931. The car is heading for the Charlestown (Main St.) Bridge rather than using the more usual routing over the Warren Bridge. *Boston Elevated Railway*

The Middlesex & Boston Street Railway and its predecessor lines ran over Boston Elevated tracks from Lake St. to Park Street Station. Car 119 of the Commonwealth Avenue Street Railway heads outbound for Auburndale by the Boston Public Library at Copley Square in the early 1900s. This photograph was the basis of a hand-colored postcard published by Raphael Tuck & Sons prior to 1907. *R. F. Turnbull, photographer; N. D. Clark Collection*

enue Street Railway were more than willing to establish such service but it was not until Saturday, January 17, 1903, that it could be inaugurated. However, instead of following the route via Beacon St., Chestnut Hill Ave. and Commonwealth Ave. specified in the operating contract, the through cars appear to have been run via Commonwealth Ave. all the way from the present Kenmore Square to Lake St. BERy crews ran the cars between Park Street Station and the Newton boundary (on Commonwealth Ave. at Lake St.) and the trolleys were operated the rest of the way by conductors and motormen of the Commonwealth Avenue company, which was consolidated on January 1, 1904, with the Newton Street Railway. The latter, in turn, was absorbed by the Middlesex & Boston Street Railway in 1909.

Started on Saturday, February 23, 1903, was the operation of through trips between Park Street Station and upper Main St., Waltham, 10½ miles, via Union Square in Allston, North Beacon St., and Watertown Square. Newton Street Railway cars were used, and were run by Boston Elevated employees between Park Street Station and Watertown Square.

The Park Street Station–Auburndale route was very heavily patronized in summer when Norumbega Park was open and the through service was continued until November 1, 1914, just a few weeks after the opening of the Boylston Street Subway. Thereafter Middlesex & Boston cars were run only between Lake St. and Auburndale, connections being made at the former point with Boston Elevated trolleys. This arrangement continued until the M&B substituted buses for trolleys on its Lake St.–Auburndale line in 1930.

The Park Street–Waltham route survived until April 1912, when service between Waltham and Central Square, Cambridge, via Watertown Square was started via the BERy and the M&B. Connections were made at Central Square with trains in the newly opened Cambridge Subway. Waltham–Cambridge trips were discontinued November 1, 1915, and thereafter M&B cars were run only between Waltham and Watertown Square, connecting with the Park Street Station–Watertown cars of the Boston Elevated.

For a brief period in March and April of 1910 the Middlesex & Boston operated so-called "Suburban Limited" trips between Park Street Station and South Framingham, 20¼ miles, via Auburndale, Newton Lower Falls, Wellesley Hills, Wellesley, and Natick. This service attracted few riders and was discontinued just a few weeks after it was started. (A similar service to Natick and Framingham had operated briefly in 1903.) Through service between Park Street Station and Newton Highlands was inaugurated as a joint route of the Boston Elevated and Middlesex & Boston on May 1, 1912, and lasted until the opening of the Boylston Street Subway in 1914. Thereafter, the M&B provided local service between Lake St. and the Highlands via Commonwealth Ave. and Walnut St.

Subway Modifications and Extensions

THE EAST BOSTON TUNNEL from Maverick Square to Court Street Station, located adjacent to Scollay Square Station, opened December 30, 1904. A new passageway, which connected the Court Street and Scollay Square Stations, was opened at this time, and it was heavily used from the start. The East Boston Tunnel was extended, starting in 1912, to Bowdoin Station and the surface incline at North Russell St. Court Street Station continued in service until November 15, 1914, at which time the passageway was closed. The extension opened March 18, 1916, and included a second new station, Scollay Under, which was connected by stairways to original Scollay Square Station above. As part of the work, this Tremont Street Subway station was expanded on the westerly side to increase the size of the center platform.

To provide a connection between Haymarket Station and Union-Friend Station on the Main Line Elevated, Haymarket was enlarged, beginning on November 29, 1908, and ending on May 23, 1909. A new wall on the west side of the station had been partially built in 1907 in anticipation of future station expansion.

On June 1, 1912, the ornamental concrete East Cambridge Viaduct over the Charles River from the Lechmere section of East Cambridge, and a companion steel elevated structure

The legislation authorizing the East Boston Tunnel provided for its connection with the Tremont Street Subway at Scollay Square. While some people argued for a physical connection between the lines, the Boston Transit Commission opted for a station at Court Street (left) adjacent to the existing subway. Passengers from the new line could enter Scollay Square Station using a special stairway (below). These views were taken in late 1904, shortly before the line opened. Court Street Station was closed in 1914 when work on an extension of the East Boston line under Scollay Square to Bowdoin Square began, but it still exists on the other side of the easterly wall of Government Center Station. *Both, Boston Transit Commission*

through Boston's West End to the Haymarket subway portal were opened. This improvement removed Somerville and East Cambridge cars from the Charles River Dam Bridge and from several streets in Boston's West End, resulting in a ten to fifteen minute cut in running time in both directions. The Boston Elevated Railway had begun construction on this extension almost five years earlier, on June 20, 1907.

The elevated structure included a seldom-used cutback, the Lowell Street Siding. After years of little use, it was extensively rehabilitated in 1948 for PCC cars and refurbished center-entrance cars to serve Boston Garden fans. Used only sparingly from the mid-1950s, it was finally taken up in the late 1980s.

The need for rapid transit service in the congested Back Bay area of Boston led to construction of the Boylston Street Subway. Work began in March 1912 on the two-track tube, which would run from a portal in Governor Square (now Kenmore Square) to an underground connection with the original Tremont Street Subway near the Public Garden Incline. The subway was routed under Commonwealth Ave. from Governor Square to the Muddy River, crossing underneath the river and running to a point beneath the intersection of Newbury St. and Charlesgate East. The line then ran under Newbury St. to Massachusetts Station, which was located at the junction of Massachusetts Ave. and Newbury St. The subway continued, parallel to the Boston & Albany Railroad main line, to Boylston St., and followed Boylston St. to Copley Station at Copley Square. From here the tunnel ran under Boylston St., joining up with the Tremont St. subway under Boylston St. adjacent to the old Public Garden Incline, and alongside a new one. During the subway construction, the incline location was shifted from the Public Garden to the middle of Boylston St., beside its

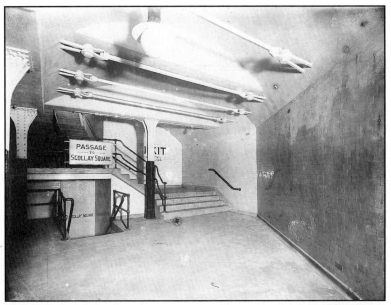

original location. The Boylston Street subway opened on October 3, 1914.

The easterly terminus of the Boylston Street Subway was not fixed initially, but Post Office Square was strongly favored. Several routes were planned. One scheme, starting at Arlington and Boylston Sts., principally followed Boylston, Essex, Kingston, and Devonshire Sts. to Post Office Square, where the subway would loop around the Post Office. Under this plan, stations were located at Boylston and Tremont Sts., Summer and Kingston Sts., and Post Office Square. Eventually, costs were deemed too high to build to Post Office Square. The plans were dropped, and the much less expensive connection with the Tremont Street Subway was substituted.

The original legislation for the Boylston Street Subway was passed in 1907, and specified that the facility would be built under the Charles River Embankment. It would be named the Riverbank Subway. Stations would be located at Charles

East Cambridge Viaduct

The East Cambridge Viaduct, now called the Lechmere Viaduct, opened in 1912. Built entirely by the Boston Elevated without a general contractor, the graceful concrete arches (above) were designed to blend with other improvements to the Charles River Basin area. The viaduct began at the Haymarket portal (left), where new ramps brought the outer tracks exiting the subway up on either side of the rails leading to Causeway St. to an elevated structure which snaked through the West End to reach the Charles River. Note the elevated train descending on its own ramp into the Washington Street Tunnel in this view taken during final testing of the new facility in May 1912. *Both, Boston Elevated Railway*

Prior to the opening of the viaduct, surface cars regularly ran over the Charles River Dam from East Cambridge to downtown Boston, entering the subway at Canal St. The opening of the structure speeded up service tremendously. In this view, the car on the viaduct has just crossed the Strauss trunnion drawbridge which spanned the channel adjacent to the dam locks. *Boston Elevated Railway*

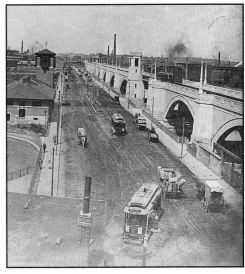

Boylston Street Subway

During construction of the Boylston Street Subway streetcars were rerouted off Boylston St. onto St. James Ave. This scene in Copley Square was taken about 1913 and shows the streetcar traffic density that the new subway would handle. The Copley Plaza Hotel, new in 1912, is on the right, and Trinity Church is to the left. *Boston Elevated Railway*

With the opening of the Boylston Street Subway in 1914, the incline for surface cars in the Public Garden was closed and a new incline was opened in the middle of Boylston St. In this view of the new portal, landscaping of the former incline area in the Garden to the left has yet to be accomplished. The Boylston Street incline was last used by Huntington Ave. cars in 1941. *Boston Transit Commission*

Although most of the entrances to the new Boylston Street Subway were of a simple design, the ornate entrance to the eastbound platform at Copley Station was intended to be architecturally compatible with the landmark McKim Building of the Boston Public Library. Copley was the one station on the new line where no exchange was possible between inbound and outbound cars since the platforms were offset from each other. *Boston Transit Commission*

In anticipation of the increase in patronage at Park Street Station with the opening of the Cambridge Subway interchange then under construction below it, the General Court in 1911 authorized the enlargement of the Tremont Street Subway station. This view taken on July 15, 1915, shows the enlarged station looking south on what was termed the "easterly" (northbound) platform. In 1936, to relieve overcrowding, the wall at left would be removed to add an additional platform and access to the Cambridge Subway exits to Tremont St. at Temple Place. *Boston Transit Commission*

St., Dartmouth St., and Massachusetts Ave., with a loop terminal adjacent to Park Street Station. The Boston Elevated Railway strongly opposed the location of the Riverbank Subway, and abutting property owners, worried about effects that the construction of the subway would have on sewers and other underground utilities, joined the company and protested to the General Court. In 1911, the lawmakers abandoned the Riverbank Subway in favor of the routing under Boylston St.

With the opening of the Cambridge Subway in 1912, Park Street Station had become the busiest station on the system. To increase the capacity of the station, the Boston Transit Commission lengthened it about 481 feet in a southerly direction. The old station platform had ended at about the location of the former Park Street Information Booth. This work was started August 7, 1914, and was completed March 8, 1915.

The famous Park Street Information Booth was opened September 15, 1923. This Boston landmark replaced earlier facilities which had been located at approximately the same location ever since the subway opened. It continued in operation until June 21, 1996.

Only a few years after the opening of the Boylston Street Subway in 1914, it became apparent that an intermediate station in the long stretch of tunnel between Boylston and Copley was needed. Wartime material restrictions delayed ac-

tion until August 15, 1919, when the Boston Transit Department began construction of Arlington Street Station, with entrances at both Arlington and Berkley Sts. The station opened for business on November 13, 1921.

The Tremont Street Subway, as originally constructed, was largely unsignaled, being essentially run as a surface streetcar line, with motormen operating their cars by line of sight. The introduction of speedy elevated trains in 1901 changed this picture dramatically, requiring a substantial system of automatic block signals. When the trains were withdrawn in 1908, the Boston Elevated decided to retain part of the signal system in a somewhat simpler form. Over the years, more signals were added, and by the mid-1920s the subway was signalized to its present-day level. The use of signals was important for successful train operation, and the introduction of trains of center-entrance cars spurred the Boston Elevated to increase the pace of signal installation.

Arlington Street Station was opened in 1921, well after the rest of the original Boylston Street Subway, when it was realized that the gap between Boylston and Copley was too great and an intermediate station was needed. This September 1937 view shows the tile work finishes common in subway stations until the start of the station modernization program in the mid-1960s. *Boston Elevated Railway*

The opening of Lechmere Station in 1922 made subway operations much more reliable. Cars from the lines at this end of the system ended their runs here, and no longer brought the delays caused by street traffic into the subway. This photo was taken on June 7, 1922, about a month before the station opened. Here a test center-entrance car waits in the station while a surface car runs outbound toward another outbound car on Bridge St. Although plans have been put forth from time to time to relocate the station to the right of the coal yard seen here and extend the tracks toward Medford, nothing has come of them to date and Lechmere remains the northerly terminus of the Green Line system. *Boston Elevated Railway*

The opening of Lechmere Terminal on July 10, 1922, greatly speeded up service in the Tremont Street Subway. Lechmere was designed as a transfer station, a point at which cars from other lines ended their trips. Passengers then transferred to a rapid transit line. The advantage of this was that delays caused by street traffic could no longer impact subway service. Single surface streetcars from the heavily-congested streets of Cambridge and Somerville now transferred their passengers to three-car trains of center-entrance cars, which were placed in service at this time. This capacity of the subway was also increased in the process. Lechmere Terminal was completely built and funded by the Boston Elevated Railway Company.

Until 1932, streetcars for the lines on Beacon St. and Commonwealth Ave. exited the Boylston Street Subway at Kenmore St. into a surface transfer station known as Kenmore Station, located just east of what was then known as Governor Square. Traffic congestion was a steadily growing problem in busy Governor Square, where streetcars and automotive traffic from Beacon St. and Commonwealth Ave. converged with more automobiles from Brookline Ave. More than 100,000 daily transit riders were constantly delayed by this congestion.

To remove streetcars from the traffic mix, on July 21, 1930, the Boston Transit Department began construction of Kenmore subway station below the surface transfer station, including an underground loop connecting the inbound and outbound Beacon Street tracks, and two subway extensions. These consisted of tunnels from the new Kenmore subway station to St. Mary's St. on the Beacon St. line, and a second tunnel from the subway station to Blandford St., near Boston University, on the Commonwealth Ave. line. This project was completed and opened for revenue service on October 23, 1932. While the subway construction was underway, the name of the square was officially changed to Kenmore Square.

In anticipation of possible conversion of the subway to third-rail rapid transit operation, the center tracks through Kenmore, which serve the Commonwealth Ave. line, were constructed on platforms over track pits in the station to facilitate conversion to high-platform loading, and a loop was provided at the inbound end of the station to allow Beacon St. streetcars to turn back. In addition, the incline rails to Commonwealth Ave. were built on raised side beams above the ground to facilitate extension of the subway west on Commonwealth Ave. The hollow part of this incline was filled in, however, during Green Line reconstruction work in the 1980s.

On January 8, 1936, a Works Progress Administration (WPA) funded project began on a new northbound platform on the through track to Scollay Square at Park Street Station, to permit right-hand boarding. This platform and connecting entrances to the street opened December 5, 1936.

In the late 1920s the elaborate kiosks at Adams Square and Scollay Square gave way to simple open stairways (similar to those used for the Arlington Street Station a few years earlier), intended to improve surface traffic visibility. In this February 1932 view, surface tracks used over the years by night cars remain, but soon these, too, will be gone. *Boston Elevated Railway*

An outbound Type 4 car and center-entrance trailer stop in Kenmore Station in November 1920. This scene would be repeated for another 12 years until the extensions to St. Mary's St. on the Beacon St. line and to Blandford St. on the Commonwealth Ave. line were opened. *Boston Elevated Railway*

Kenmore Extension

In this view taken on July 15, 1931, the photographer is right beside the Governor Square portal, looking toward Kenmore Square. Excavation of the Kenmore subway station is well underway, and the impact of the construction is obviously enormous. *Boston Elevated Railway*

The incline to Commonwealth Ave. near Blandford St. featured decking over an extension of the subway shell, which had been purposely built to expedite further extension of the subway to the west under Commonwealth Ave. The planks are clearly shown in this August 1934 view. *Boston Elevated Railway*

Huntington Avenue Subway construction was getting started in this view (above) at Northeastern University, taken in 1937. As the subway was built, the Huntington Ave. car line continued uninterrupted on temporary decking above the excavation. The ceremonial first train (right) entered the new subway on February 16, 1941. *Above, Boston Elevated Railway; right, Stanley M. Hauck, Carlson Collection*

On September 18, 1937, the Boston Transit Department began the Huntington Avenue Subway. This was also a WPA program, but a much larger one than the Park Street Station expansion, and was one of the first examples of major federal funding for local mass transit construction. This subway extension opened on February 16, 1941. The new tunnel started just west of Copley Station near Exeter St. and left the main subway at grade. This switch is known today as Copley Junction. The line turned left under Exeter St., then right under Huntington Ave., running to Mechanics Station, located at Huntington Ave. and West Newton St. near the Mechanics Hall. From Mechanics, the line continued to Symphony Station, at Massachusetts and Huntington Aves., adjacent to Symphony Hall. Here the subway was placed on either side of a new road underpass carrying Huntington Ave. traffic under Massachusetts Ave. Leaving Symphony, cars entered the incline to Northeastern University almost immediately.

The incline tracks of this subway were also supported on raised side beams, in a way similar to the Commonwealth Ave. incline, for possible extension of the subway on Huntington Ave. In fact, the subway shell extended full-depth as far as Opera Place, and was located under and near the end of the existing Northeastern University stop. As part of Green Line reconstruction in the 1980s, the MBTA filled in both the hollow section of the Northeastern incline and the extension to Opera Place.

Prior to the subway, the Huntington Ave. car line ran past Northeastern University to Copley Square, and then over Boylston St. as far as the block between Arlington and Charles Sts. Here, the streetcars entered the portal to the Boylston Street Subway. The Huntington Ave. line was the last major surface streetcar route to run through this heavily congested section of the Back Bay, and its diversion to the new subway on February 16, 1941, shortened the running time considerably and brought large numbers of new riders.

Postwar Changes

UNTIL THE LATE 1940s, two lines ran from Charlestown on the north between Sullivan Square Station and Brattle Street Loop, where there was a separate platform located adjacent to the Scollay Square Station. These lines ran from Sullivan to Brattle via Main St., Charlestown, and via Bunker Hill St., Charlestown, respectively. They were local fare routes, and passengers going from the Brattle platform to the Scollay platform were required to pay an additional fare because Scollay was a prepayment area and Brattle was not. The Main St. line was converted to buses on April 3, 1948, and the Bunker Hill St. route followed on July 2, 1949.

Both lines entered the subway system from Causeway St. at the Canal Street Loop and proceeded directly into the subway through the Haymarket portal. Between Canal Street and Brattle, cars from both lines ran on the two center subway tracks all the way to Brattle; this trackage was exclusively devoted to their use. To replace the subway service that was lost after the Charlestown car lines were abandoned, and to continue to provide a connection to buses from Charlestown, the MTA began operating a single-car shuttle between North Station and Brattle Street on October 15, 1949. The car loaded on unused trackage on the Haverhill St. side of the North Station Loop rather than on the Canal St. side. Beginning on December 1, 1951, the shuttle was operated weekdays only, between 4:10 p.m. and 5:55 p.m. It was discontinued completely in September 1952, and was the last regularly scheduled streetcar service on the northerly center tracks of the subway.

Until March 2, 1953, the City Point–North Station line from South Boston via Broadway entered the portal at Tremont St. and Broadway. This line used a specialized flying junction inside the portal at Tremont St. and Broadway to join the car line coming to and from Egleston Square. Soon after the City Point service was discontinued, the MTA eliminated the four-

The short-lived shuttle operation between Boylston Street Station and the Broadway portal was the last operation through this section of the subway. A shuttle car is seen at the Broadway end of the line in February 1962. *Edward A. Anderson*

Not all changes in the 1950s and early 1960s were negative. Science Park Station opened on the Lechmere Viaduct in 1955. In November 1976 a two-car train leaves the elevated station for Lechmere. *Stephen P. Carlson*

track exit from this portal and converted it to two tracks, using the remaining space for a bus transfer station adjacent to the portal. The work consisted of removing the inbound and outbound rails from the South Boston incline and connecting the Tremont inbound and outbound rails in their place. This allowed the area formerly used by the Tremont rails to be used for a bus waiting area adjacent to the Tremont St. sidewalk, and for steps and a landing leading down to another platform to be constructed for passenger transfer to the outbound Egleston cars. This work took place between September 25 and November 24, 1953.

Science Park Station was added to the Lechmere Viaduct in 1955, opening on August 20. The station served the Museum of Science and residents of Boston's West End.

When the Riverside Line was opened in 1959, a new connection to the subway was built between St. Mary's St. and Kenmore Station. This led to a new ramp and portal near Park Drive, between Beacon and Boylston Sts. Fenway Park Station on the new line was also located at this point.

On November 18, 1961, the Metropolitan Transit Authority abandoned the North Station–Lenox St. car line, the last subway-surface route through the section of the Tremont Street Subway between Boylston Station and Broadway. For several more months, the MTA ran a shuttle service from Boylston Station to the portal at Broadway and Tremont St., but this was eventually dropped on April 6, 1962.

Subway service was severely affected on October 6, 1962, when the Muddy River in the Fenway overflowed, flooding Kenmore Station, and in the process interrupting streetcar service on the Beacon, Commonwealth, and Riverside lines until October 11. Buses were pressed into service on the affected lines while the MTA pumped out the water and made repairs.

Another stretch of the original Tremont Street Subway was abandoned on October 28, 1963. At this time, the northbound subway tube between Scollay Square and Haymarket Station, which ran under Cornhill St. and a section of Washington St. including Adams Square Station, was abandoned. This was replaced by a new northbound tunnel bore to Haymarket. At the same time, a turnback loop for cars coming from Park Street was installed. Reflecting changes aboveground, the Scollay Square Station was renamed Government Center.

In October 1964 the outer loop at Park Street Station was removed. A switch was installed between the southbound through track and the inner loop so that cars from Government Center could use the inner track at Park Street.

On August 26, 1965, the Tremont Street Subway, the Boylston Street Subway, the Huntington Avenue Subway, and their connecting surface lines were officially designated the Green Line as part of the MBTA's new color-coding scheme. At that same time, the five routes then feeding into

PCC car 3268 loads for Lechmere at Adams Square Station on March 22, 1963. This station was closed late at night and on Sundays for budgetary reasons for most of the last decade it was in operation. *Edward A. Anderson*

New subway construction in the late 1950s involved creation of a short segment from an at-grade junction in the Beacon St. branch of the Kenmore Extension to the surface near Fenway Park and a link with the Highland Branch. Contemporary MBTA Type 7 car 3624 emerges from the Fenway Park portal in late December 1986. This portal has twice been the gateway for the Muddy River to inundate the subway. *Stephen P. Carlson*

the subway—Watertown, Boston College, Cleveland Circle, Riverside, and Arborway—were designated by the letters A to E, respectively. Although appearing soon thereafter on system maps and timetables, these route letters did not show up on car destination signs until the arrival of the Boeing LRVs in the mid-1970s.

Starting in 1969, a new Haymarket Station was built as a two-track facility with an island platform. The new station opened May 10, 1971, and was located south of the old 4-track Haymarket Station, which was abandoned.

On June 21, 1969, a long-lived Green Line branch, A-*Watertown*, was discontinued. At this time, buses were introduced on the line, running from Watertown Carhouse to the Kenmore busway, on an experimental basis, but the change eventually became permanent. For many years, the Watertown Carbarn was used for the repair of work cars and badly-damaged Green Line streetcars, and for the storage of obsolete equipment. The track connection to the subway at Packards Corner (Commonwealth and Brighton Aves.) remained intact, and the line was live as late as 1994. In 1996, removal of the car tracks began, and as of this writing, the work is largely complete. A short section of track for disabled cars remains on Brighton Ave. at Packards Corner.

(Watertown–Park Street was an old line, and it came into being in pieces. The segment of the route between Oak Square, Brighton, and Union Square, Allston, began operation as part of a horsecar route from Oak Square to Bowdoin Square in downtown Boston on November 15, 1858. This was also part of a branch off Boston's first electric line on Beacon St. in Brookline. Electric cars began regular operation from Allston to Park Square on January 3, 1889, and from Oak Square on January 13. New track on Commonwealth and Brighton Aves. from Beacon St. at Kenmore Square was completed May 18, 1896. Track on Washington St., Park St., and Tremont St. in Newton, as well as Tremont St. in Brighton to Oak Square, was also complete by this time, and a short time later, on June 13, 1896, a new electric line began running from Nonantum Square (Newton Corner today), Newton, to North Union Station in downtown Boston. On August 4, 1900, this line was extended on the outer end from Nonantum Square to Watertown Square, along Galen St., finally creating the surface trackage part of the A-Line. Through service from Watertown to the subway took a while to start, but by 1912, the A-Line was running from Watertown to Park Street.)

Canal Street Loop at North Station was converted to a stub-end facility for double-end cars, closing on June 18, 1977, and reopening after the conversion on December 15 that same year. The Canal Street stub-end terminal was closed completely on March 28, 1997, to make way for the extension of the Tremont St. subway under the terminal area and North Station. This new subway segment will replace the steel elevated structure from the Haymarket portal over Causeway St. and Lomasney Way, and beside Martha Rd., to a point just south of Science Park Station.

A Type 7 car emerges from the trackage to the Canal Street Loop on March 23, 1997. This trackage was abandoned five days later to make way for the extension of the original Tremont Street Subway in a new tunnel under North Station with a new connecting ramp to the Lechmere Viaduct. To the rights are new temporary tracks and an elevated structure to allow removal of the old ramps into the Haymarket portal, also for the new tunnel. Interestingly, the new elevated structure runs over almost the same alignment that the Charlestown Elevated did in this area until 1975. *Bradley H. Clarke*

The Tremont Street Subway does what it was designed to do: move large masses of people efficiently through downtown Boston. This scene at Park Street Station dates from the 1950s. *Silloway Collection*

On March 9, 1979, a passageway connecting the northbound Park Street Green Line platform with the southbound Washington Street Station Orange Line platform (formerly Winter Street Station) was opened to the public. This was the final part of a modernization project at Park Street Station. It had been built as part of Section A of the Dorchester Tunnel, which was opened on April 4, 1915. Dubbed the Winter Street Concourse, the passageway was intended to connect the Park Street and Winter Street Station ticket lobbies, but lay dormant for years, setting the stage for this curious opening 64 years after completion!

Beginning in March 1980 with the reconstruction of the E-*Arborway* Huntington Ave. streetcar median and subway trackage, and continuing through 1989, with the reopening of the E-Line street trackage from Brigham Circle to Heath Street Loop on November 4, much of the Green Line track bed and power distribution system was rebuilt. The completion of the Huntington Ave. work late in 1980 was followed in June 1982 with the reconstruction of Reservoir Carhouse, a project that ended in July 1984, and in July 1982 with the rebuilding of the C-*Cleveland Circle* line, which was finished in September of that year. From July through November 1983, reconstruction of large sections of the B-*Boston College* line took place. From June 1985 through December 1988, most of the subway facilities from Kenmore to Lechmere were rebuilt as well. Buses generally provided service on the sections of the lines that were affected by construction activity.

The Muddy River revisited the subway on October 20, 1996, when unusually heavy rains produced severe flooding. Water again flowed down the Fenway Park ramp and filled Kenmore Station. Unlike the 1962 incident, however, the remainder of the subway almost as far as Boylston Street, including parts of the Highland Branch and E-*Heath* line, was flooded. Full operation resumed in stages; not until October 27 were all lines back in operation. Considerable busing was required during this period. It took several additional months before signal systems could be replaced and services could be run at normal speeds and schedules.

Subway Rolling Stock

MUCH OF THE FALL, WINTER, AND SPRING SERVICE in the Tremont Street Subway from 1897 through 1907 was provided by 25-foot double-truck closed cars, of which the West End Street Railway and the Boston Elevated purchased or built 1,202 from 1890 through 1900. Seating 34 passengers, they weren't very fast because they had only two motors, but they proved adequate until the acquisition of larger cars began in 1904.

The first air-braked surface cars on the Boston Elevated system were 60 cars with 26½-foot bodies ordered in 1903 and delivered early in 1904. They were placed in service in the Tremont Street Subway in February of that year and were run from Park Street Station to Newton via Brighton, and on the present Green Line routes to Cleveland Circle and Boston College. For about two years, beginning in the fall of 1905, six cars were equipped to haul 25-foot closed cars as trailers between Park Street Station and Oak Square, Brighton.

Nearly 750 opens of the 9-bench type, each seating 45 passengers, were acquired by the West End and Boston Elevated from 1893 through 1899. These were the major type of summer car on the system for many years. It fell to car 1752 of this type (*see page 20*) to make the first revenue run in the Tremont Street Subway. Operated in the subway and on many surface lines, they were being run on nearly 80 routes as late as 1911. Retirements began in 1919 and the very last was burned for scrap in 1923.

The acquisition of double-truck semi-convertibles with air brakes and either two or four motors each was started by the Boston Elevated in 1905, and 190 were on the property by the end of 1908. There were three major groups: the Type 1s (5001-5040), the Type 2s (5041-5091), and the Type 3s (5091-5190), and cars of the two latter groups were in service in the Tremont Street Subway at various times, running on some of the longer routes originating at Park Street Station.

The most common closed streetcar in Boston in the 1890s had a 25-foot body. Car 787 of that type (center) operates with several others on temporary track over the roof of the subway at Park Street Station on November 10, 1896. The diversion was necessary as the tunnel construction shifted from under the Boston Common mall to Tremont St. itself. *Boston Transit Commission*

Familiar sights in the Tremont Street Subway from late 1911 through the World War II years were the Type 4 semi-convertibles of the Boston Elevated. There were 275 of these, Nos. 5191-5465, ordered from four builders from 1910 through 1913, and they were assigned for many years to the principal subway-surface routes of the system. They had a seating capacity of 52 and all were equipped during the 1915-19 period to draw center-entrance trailers. Revamping of the cars for one-man operation commenced in 1922. Retirements began in 1944 and the last 22, all in wretched condition, were sold for scrap in September 1952.

Possibly the most efficient rolling stock ever operated in the Tremont Street Subway were the 405 center-entrance motor cars acquired by the Boston Elevated Railway from 1916 through 1920. Three hundred of these, Nos. 6000-6299, were equipped for operation in trains of up to three cars, while Nos. 6300-6404 were run as single units. They had a seating capacity of 56 but there was plenty of room for standees and the cars were very effective in handling large crowds. Some were scrapped as early as 1937 but 232 remained at the end of 1940 and 148 were on hand at the end of 1945. The last 26 were retired in 1953.

Type 3 No. 5155 leaves North Station West for Clarendon Hill in Somerville in June 1912. This was one of the so-called "semi-convertible" cars acquired between 1905 and 1913. A Type 4 car loads far down on the inbound platform for the Tremont Street Subway. *Boston Elevated Railway*

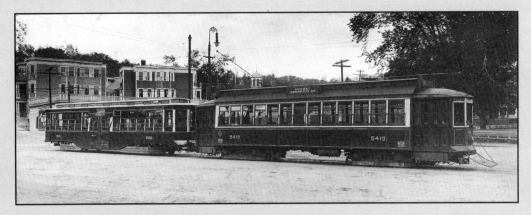

A train consisting of Type 4 No. 5419 and center-entrance trailer No. 7001 is seen in 1915 at Oak Square, Brighton, running on the Newton Corner–Park Street Subway line. *Boston Elevated Railway*

Service over the Sullivan Square–Brattle Street Loop routes via Main St. and via Bunker Hill St. was provided for many years by Type 5 semi-convertibles, of which 471 were purchased by the Boston Elevated during the 1922-1927 period. These lines were motorized in 1948 and 1949 respectively, but 48 Type 5s were equipped in 1950-52 with Tomlinson automatic couplers so they could be operated on the Park Street Station–Northeastern University and Park Street–Heath Street lines. These were replaced by double-end PCC cars acquired from Dallas, Texas, in 1958-59, and retired.

The Tremont Street Subway had seen its initial PCCs, however, on March 3, 1941, when the first of 20 cars, Nos. 3002-3021, were placed in service on the Brighton-Newton-Watertown line. Between 1944 and 1946, 250 additional cars, Nos. 3022-3271, all equipped for multiple-unit operation, were in service on the Beacon St., Huntington Ave., Tremont St., and South Boston subway-surface lines. More new PCCs (3272-3321) were added in 1951, and their advent spelled the doom of the last Type 4s and center-entrance cars.

The PCCs reigned supreme in the subway until the debut of the Boeing-Vertol light rail vehicles (LRVs) in 1976-78 and then were swiftly phased out. The 11 still active are assigned to the non-subway Mattapan–Ashmont route.

The Boeing-Vertol LRVs, of which 144 (3400-3543) were delivered starting in 1976, were the first new rolling stock ordered for the Green Line since 1951. The original order was for 175 cars, but design problems resulted in the MBTA canceling part of the order. Fifty-five cars were rebuilt in 1996-97, and a total of 65 LRVs remain in service today.

A new streetcar design, the Type 7, was conceived in the early 1980s, and 100 of these cars (3600-3699) were built for the MBTA by Kinki-Sharyo of Japan and delivered between 1986 and 1988. An additional 20 cars (3700-3719) were delivered in 1997. This fleet has been extremely reliable and is well-liked by the riding public. Current plans call for the fleet to be electrically modified to run in trains with the new Type 8 cars.

Recently, the MBTA ordered 100 new cars for the Green Line from Breda, in Milan, Italy. The Type 8 cars (3800-3899) will feature low floor design for easy boarding and alighting, and will incorporate AC electric motors, a first for the Green Line. A prototype is expected in January 1998, and the first production cars should begin arriving in 1998-99.

The large center doors on the center-entrance cars made them ideal for swallowing crowds in the subway. No. 6298 operates through Copley Square on its way to the Arborway about 1938. Following is Type 4 No. 5230 on a run to the Francis St. crossover. *Seashore Trolley Museum Collection*

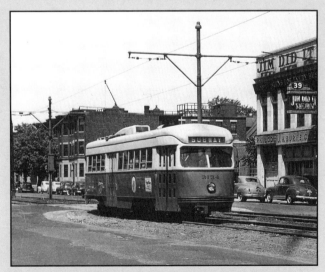

No car type served the Tremont Street Subway longer than the PCC. On June 4, 1949, PCC 3134 proceeds along Brighton Ave. on its journey from Watertown to Park Street Station. The Watertown line was "temporarily" bused in 1969, and finally torn up in the mid-1990s. *Norton D. Clark, Clarke Collection*

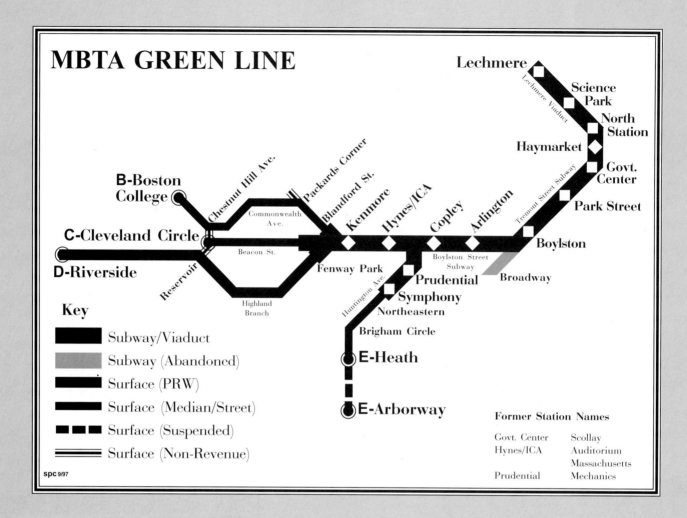

Current Green Line services are operated with two types of cars. The oldest are the Boeing-Vertol LRVs, the first of which entered service in late 1976. Car 3509, seen in the snow at Riverside in March 1978, was wrecked in an accident at North Station on April 24, 1979. *Norton D. Clark, Carlson Collection*

Like the LRV, the Type 7 is a two-section articulated vehicle. A two-car train headed by 3612 makes its way toward Lake St. in 1989. The Type 7 fleet provided the bulk of the 142 cars required for rush-hour service on the Green Line in the spring of 1997. *Bradley H. Clarke*

The Green Line Branches

OVER THE PAST 100 YEARS, numerous surface lines have fed into the Tremont Street Subway and its extensions. A full history of all such routes is beyond the scope of this book. This section provides brief profiles of the four lines currently providing service in the subway. It should be noted that the downtown terminals of each line have changed from time to time in response to operational needs; no attempt has been made to record all such variations here.

C-*Cleveland Circle*
The Beacon St. Line

THE BEACON ST. LINE was one of the original lines which ran into the Tremont Street Subway. The Beacon St. line is the oldest operating streetcar line in Massachusetts, and was the second electric streetcar line to operate in the state. It is also the oldest operating electric streetcar line in America. Since this line was the first electric line in Boston, its early history is significant and we will cover this line in more depth than the other Green Line branches.

Late in 1887, Henry M. Whitney, president of the West End Street Railway, had completed the merger of his company and the competing horse railroads. He could focus of his main priority now—the completion of his flagship, the Beacon St. line. Whitney had a closely-related second priority, though, and this was embodied in the universal desire of the street railway industry to replace the horse as a source of motive power. This need for new technology became inextricably interwoven with the Beacon St. line and would change forever the future development of the street railway industry.

On December 28, 1886, the selectmen of Brookline granted the West End Street Railway Company the right to lay tracks on Beacon, Harvard, and Washington Sts. The company said

Henry M. Whitney was the man who brought the electric streetcar to Boston. *J. A. J. Wilcox, Clarke Collection*

that it intended to open the line using horsecars. However, in appearing before the Brookline Selectmen, Henry Whitney stated there was little doubt that "electricity will generally be adopted, but as of yet, it has not passed the experimental stage." Track construction began on August 20, 1887, at the corner of Beacon and Charles Sts. in Brookline. Progress was slow and in March 1888 the West End petitioned the town of Brookline to extend the opening date of the Beacon St. line from April 1 to June 1, 1888. This request was granted. As of

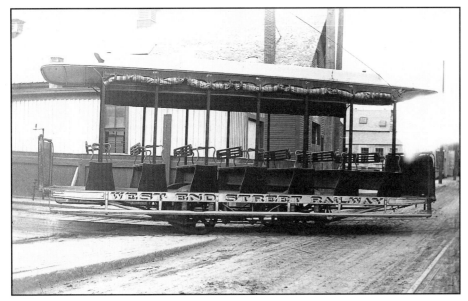

Henry Whitney's West End Street Railway consolidated nearly all streetcar operations in Boston under a single management. Few of the company's cars carried its name, being painted for their routes instead. This open horsecar, posed sans horse on South St. at Jamaica Plain Station about 1891, is an exception. *West End Street Railway*

April 28, 1888, the Beacon St. trackage was complete from West Chester Park (Massachusetts Ave.) in Boston to Harvard St. in Brookline.

On Friday morning, June 1, 1888, the first horsecar operated over the new Beacon St. route. Service initially was sporadic. The company had wanted to run its primary and newest route with electric cars, but this would not happen for another seven months. Meanwhile, the Lynn & Boston Street Railway Company, on November 19, 1888, began operation of electric streetcars on the Highland Circuit route in Lynn. This was the first electric trolley line in Massachusetts.

Electrically-propelled trolley cars had emerged in a few cities by this time, and Whitney wanted to take a closer look. A newly-built trolley system in Richmond, Virginia, with 12 miles of track, looked promising. The Richmond system had opened on February 2, 1888, and had been built with equipment furnished by a company formed by Frank Julian Sprague, now known as the "Father of Electric Traction." After several agonizing months of equipment shakedowns, by late spring of 1888 the system was operating reliably and attracting national attention.

Whitney visited Richmond. After several convincing technical demonstrations by Frank Sprague and Richmond company officials, Whitney was satisfied that the trolley car would be the right choice for Beacon St. and probably the preferred replacement for horse cars on the entire West End Street Railway system. Whitney next visited a Bentley-Knight Electric Railway Company installation in Allegheny City, Pennsylvania, and a Thompson-Houston Electric Company line in Washington, D.C. Richmond impressed Whitney the most. The Sprague Electric Railway & Motor Company was awarded a large contract on July 17, 1888, to demonstrate its technology on the Beacon St. line.

On July 16, 1888, the Brookline selectmen held a particularly important public hearing on the petition of the West End Street Railway for leave "to erect, maintain and use an 'electric system' of motive power in the operation of its cars" on Beacon St., Harvard St., and Longwood Ave. At the hearing, Henry Whitney extolled the virtues of the trolley, adding that he could have the Beacon St. line in operation by October 1. Public reaction was favorable, and on August 13 the selectmen voted to permit overhead wires on Beacon and Harvard Sts.

On September 24, 1888, the Boston Aldermen had also granted electrification rights to the West End, but overhead wires were not permitted in the Back Bay Section of Boston east of West Chester Park. Thus, sub-surface conduits between the inner rails for current collection were required. These were built on Beacon St. from St. Mary's St. at the Brookline town line to West Chester Park, along West Chester Park to Boylston St., on Boylston St. to Park Square, then on Providence and Church Sts. back to Boylston St. Overhead trolley wire was also authorized on the section of the line from St. Mary's St. to Charlesgate East, so both systems of this new technology were permitted along this section of Beacon St. Just before the line was set to open, on December 24, 1888, the West End was granted an additional electrification right along the stretch of Beacon St. in Brighton, from the Boston-Brookline boundary to Chestnut Hill Ave.

The conduit was described in some detail in the *Boston Journal* for December 31, 1888. It was located between the inner running rails of each track and extended about a foot below the street surface. Deep manholes designed for easy cleaning were located at frequent intervals for the removal of snow, ice, and street debris. Two parallel copper bars about 1¼ inches thick were used for current delivery and return. They were suspended in the conduit, one on each side, about 4 to 5 inches below the slot, which itself was about five-eighths of an inch wide.

The *Boston Globe* on February 5, 1889, described in detail the equipment on the cars. Two spring loaded metal strips about 10 inches square called "plows" were located on a support rail bolted to the truck frame. Each plow slid along one of the copper bars in the conduit as the car moved along, one continuously collecting traction power, and the other returning it. The plows could be easily raised and lowered to speed

One of the earliest electric cars, West End Street Railway No. 433, poses at Oak Square Carhouse in late 1888 or early 1889. Notice the lever assembly located at the center of the truck frame. This appears to be the mechanism for raising and lowering the conduit plows. The gentleman standing to the extreme left has been identified as Henry M. Whitney. *Silloway Collection*

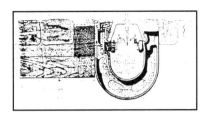

In this rare view, car 441 is on its way to Brookline at the corner of Dartmouth and Boylston Sts. in Copley Square. This was part of the section originally fed by the Bentley-Knight conduit (above), but the trolley pole in use on one of the original electric cars and the heavy clothing worn by the motorman date this photo to the winter of 1890. Henry Hobson Richardson's masterpiece Trinity Church is behind the car. *Above,* Electric Railway Journal, *Oct. 8, 1904; left, State Street Boston Corporation Art Collection*

the transition from conduit to overhead wire operation. This was done with a lever assembly found on the side of the truck frame. In the raised position, the plows were held in a horizontal position, a safety measure which made them hard to come in contact with and almost invisible.

By early October 1888 the electrification of the Beacon St. line and its branches had begun. Also, at this time, the tracks were also complete as far as Englewood Ave. (near Cleveland Circle) on a new extension from Harvard St. to the Chestnut Hill Reservoir, the location of today's Cleveland Circle.

Saturday, December 1, 1888, was especially noteworthy because the first recorded use of an electric trolley car on the West End Street Railway system happened at this time. That evening a Sprague electric car made a short run near the Oak Square carhouse on Washington St., Brighton.

Work on the conduit section held up the opening of the line. The *Boston Globe* reported on December 27, 1888, that conduit installation had been completed Saturday, December 22, and that the spaces between the slots and running rails were being filled with concrete. The article added that five cars were then equipped for both conduit and overhead wire operation, and 12 cars were outfitted for overhead wire only. Four cars had been shipped to New York for motor installation by Bentley-Knight.

The first run of a conduit car in Boston was documented in the *Boston Journal* for December 31, 1888. One round trip using the Bentley-Knight system was made on Boylston St. between Ipswich and Dartmouth Sts. on Saturday, December 29. The Beacon St. electrification was now in readiness. Last-minute connections were made, finishing touches were applied. The entire line would start electric operation almost immediately.

Late Monday evening, December 31, 1888, and into the early Tuesday morning hours of January 1, 1889, electric trolley car operation took place on the entire Beacon St. line. This was the first time that both the conduit and overhead wire systems were used for a continuous trip. Two cars were used, starting from Allston about midnight, one under the control of Frank Sprague, the other under an electrician, a Mr. Mansfield. Both cars derailed at the corner of Boylston and Church Sts. in the downtown area because of a bad piece of track, but they were returned to the rail quickly. Henry Whitney was quite pleased with this first trip, and told Sprague that he could fill both cars with interested onlookers and take them to Beacon St. or as far as he wanted. Both cars were quickly filled and were soon grinding out of town. What a way to celebrate New Year's Eve!

Overhead trolley wire was used from Oak Square to the edge of the Back Bay, and conduit was used from that point (Beacon St. and Charlesgate East) to Park Square. As opened, the conduit segment was about 1.55 miles in length, and the section under trolley wire was 2.48 miles long. West End records show that other test runs were made on January 2. The line finally opened to the public on Thursday, January 3, 1889. Cars were run half-hourly and large numbers of people rode the new line.

The line was partly out of service on January 5 because of an overheated generator bearing at the Allston Power Station. A drive belt had to be removed which had left only one generator functional, and this was insufficient for the cars to handle grades or sharp curves. Rain on January 6, 1889, kept the tracks clean all day, and the electric cars were crowded and experienced their best day yet. The only problem noted was at the end of the day, when cars were left in total darkness during a four to five minute delay each time the crews switched

Reconstruction in 1903 of the Beacon St. bridge over the Boston & Albany Railroad required the Boston Elevated to build an outbound shoe-fly track. Work in progress is delaying inbound 12-bench open No. 3221 on its way to Park St. This car was one of 60 built in BERy's Bartlett Street Shops in 1901. *Silloway Collection*

from the conduit to the overhead system.

The section of the Beacon St. line from Coolidge Corner to the Chestnut Hill Reservoir was opened on January 12, 1889, and cars began making through runs from Chestnut Hill to Park Square. As of January 19, service was half-hourly. The distance between the terminals was approximately 7.73 miles.

Regular passenger operation with electrics began over the trackage from Oak Square, Brighton, to Harvard Ave., Allston, on January 13, 1889. The through route was Oak Square–Park Square, and the one-way trip was about 6.16 miles in length. Service was half-hourly, with the first car leaving Oak Square at 5:47 a.m. and the last at 10:17 p.m. The first returning car left Park Square at 6:47 a.m. and the last at 11:17 p.m. There was mixed horsecar and electric car service, initially, but on January 19, 1889, just six days after the inauguration of electric service, the West End decided to eliminate the horsecars. Electric operations were going better than expected and company officials were fully confident in the electric operation.

West End President Henry M. Whitney personally conducted a tour of the Beacon St. line and its branches on Wednesday, January 16, 1889, for the city officials of Cambridge and their aides. The weather was stormy but many attended. The trip began at Coolidge Corner, ran to Oak Square, Brighton, and returned to Allston, where the party stopped to inspect the new power station. The tour then returned to Coolidge Corner, where the group transferred to a car for Reservoir. From there the party went on to Boston. The tour was flawless and the guests were impressed with the new operation. Afterwards Whitney took the entire party to the Algonquin Club. The trip was repeated a number of times for other curious groups of municipal and company officials.

Despite the general success of the Beacon St. electrification, there was one less-than-satisfactory aspect: conduit operation. This was a constant source of trouble, for any metallic object that dropped into the conduit slot, either by accident or deliberately, usually resulted in a short circuit and an immediate halt to service. Furthermore, thermal expansion and contraction of the slot damaged the current collector "plows," and ice formation in the slot brought still more woes. Reliable service was difficult under good weather conditions and almost impossible at inclement times.

There were also public safety considerations. In an episode reported in the April 10, 1889, edition of the *Boston Globe* in a piece entitled, "Why the Horses Shrieked," a team of horses was electrocuted while trotting over the streetcar tracks on the Boylston St. Bridge, which ran across the Boston & Albany Railroad. They fell to the ground immediately, "uttering the most piercing cries." Members of Engine Company 15 cut the traces and tried to release the horses, who continued their cries of terror. The firemen and one of their dogs also received shocks, and the horses once released dashed madly away in different directions. They were recaptured later, none the worse for their ordeal. Episodes such as this convinced the public that the conduit operation was dangerous, and popular sentiment turned against it.

The West End Street Railway acted swiftly to end this nuisance. The *Boston Journal* for March 28, 1889, reported a hearing on the previous day before the Boston Board of Aldermen on a petition of the West End to use overhead wires over all streets in Boston on which it held locations, including the section then using conduit power. Henry D. Hyde, Esq., representing the West End, said that the conduit had proved

The Beacon St. line ran in a tree-lined reservation in the center of the street. A two-car center-entrance outbound train led by No. 6215 (left) passes Englewood Ave. on its way to Cleveland Circle in the 1930s. PCCs replaced the center-entrance cars on the line. "Picture Window" No. 3277 (below) is on the way down the hill at Dean Rd. The "Gray Ghost" paint scheme was distinctive, but short-lived. *Left, Boston Elevated Railway; below, Bradley H. Clarke*

to be unreliable and a disappointment, working well occasionally, but poorly at most other times. The overhead system, however, generally performed well. On May 1, 1889, the Boston Aldermen approved the West End's request to use overhead trolley wire throughout the city, and the Mayor gave his approval on May 10.

By early July 1889 conduit operation had been discontinued, and on July 9, 1889, the overhead trolley wire system was in use over the entire route for the first time. The conversion had been delayed by the low hanging tree limbs over Boylston St. from Arlington to Charles St. The branches had interfered with the trolley poles on the streetcars because the tracks here ran on the side of the street instead of in the center. Residents proposed moving the tracks to the center of the road rather than cut the limbs, but the West End balked at spending the $10,000 needed to do this and finally got permission to trim the offending branches. The West End towed the electrics with horses on this section for a brief period between the end of the conduit operation and until the trees had been trimmed.

The Beacon St. trolley line was very popular. Ridership rose steadily, assuring the expansion of trolley service to other lines. The trolley had achieved broad public acceptance. Following the successful electrification of Beacon St. and its Allston-Brighton branch, the West End Street Railway petitioned the Brookline selectmen for permission to electrify the remaining Brookline horsecar routes, a request that was speedily granted. Following closely on the heels of the Beacon St. electrification, the second electric car line of the West End opened on February 16, 1889, between Bowdoin Square, Boston, and Harvard Square, Cambridge. The 1890s went on to be a vigorous period for street railway growth and expansion in Metropolitan Boston.

With the opening of America's first subway on September 1, 1897, Beacon St. riders immediately benefited. Cars from the Beacon St. line were routed into the new facility on opening day, a move which greatly shortened the riding time

from Brookline to the heart of the downtown area.

The ride to downtown Boston was speeded up even more on October 3, 1914, by the opening of the Boylston Street Subway to Kenmore Square, then known as Governor Square. Beacon St. and Commonwealth Ave. riders were the prime beneficiaries. Construction of Kenmore Station and two extensions of the Boylston Street Subway from Kenmore Square to Blandford St. on Commonwealth Ave. and to St. Mary's St. on the Beacon St. line was completed October 23, 1932. This freed streetcars on these two lines from the fierce traffic congestion of Kenmore Square

The Massachusetts Bay Transportation Authority took note of the one-hundredth anniversary of the electrification of Beacon St. by conducting a ceremonial ride from Reservoir Carhouse to Park Street Station on Wednesday, January 18, 1989. Officials of the MBTA, Brookline, and Boston participated. Making the trip extra special was Type 5 No. 5734, on lease to the MBTA from the Seashore Trolley Museum, which made the run down Beacon St. At Park Street Station, the MBTA commemorated the C-Line centennial with a public ceremony.

The Commonwealth Ave. line originally ended at this stub-end terminal at Lake St. This scene, taken in the late 1890s, shows the Commonwealth Avenue Street Railway's track continuing beyond the shelter to Auburndale and Norumbega Park. At this time, Boston Elevated cars were only using Commonwealth Ave. as far as Chestnut Hill Ave., and running down the latter to the Beacon St. line, hence, "Reservoir" on the side of the cars.

B-*Boston College*
The Commonwealth Ave. Line

ON AUGUST 15, 1896, an extension of the Beacon St. line was opened from Reservoir, at the line's outer end, to the Newton-Boston boundary line near Lake St., Brighton. Starting from Lake St., the extension ran over Commonwealth Ave. (then called Commonwealth Ave. Extension) and Chestnut Hill Ave. Cars then ran on Beacon St. to Beacon and Washington Sts., and then followed Washington St. through Brookline Village to downtown Boston.

A new segment of track along Commonwealth Ave. between Chestnut Hill Ave. and Brighton Ave. was opened May 26, 1900. Cars ran from Lake St. to downtown Boston over essentially the same route the Commonwealth Ave. line follows today. Today's route, however, uses the Boylston Street Subway, which was not built until 1914, with a later extension in 1932 to the present-day Blandford St. portal, as previously mentioned. Service was heavy from the start. Seventy-five trips per day were operated, with a seating capacity of 5,100 over the round-trip run of 13.026 miles. A third siding was installed at the end of the line during May 1900 in anticipation of the need for extra car storage as a result of ridership demand.

From 1903 to 1914, the Commonwealth Avenue Street Railway and its successors, the Newton Street Railway and the Middlesex & Boston Street Railway, ran service from Norumbega Park in Auburndale to Park Street Station. This route ran entirely via Commonwealth Ave. to the subway as Route 923. It started January 17, 1903. When the Boylston Street Subway was opened to Kenmore Square, on October 3, 1914, Commonwealth Ave. and Watertown cars of the Boston Elevated Railway were promptly routed into the new tube. Through service from Auburndale to Park Street was discontinued, however, on November 1, 1914. The old two-motor cars of the Middlesex & Boston Street Railway were much too slow for subway service, and were unable to keep up with the newer four-motor Type 4 cars used by the Elevated in the subway.

The Boston Braves played a World Series October 11-12, 1915, in Brighton at their field, just off the Commonwealth Ave. line. Just one week too late, the Elevated opened a loop which allowed streetcars to directly serve Braves Field, entering an area beside the field via Babcock St., and leaving on Gaffney St. Once beside the field, the tracks expanded to two to increase the crowd hauling capacity.

A prepayment area at Governor Square was opened in 1915, primarily to speed up service to Red Sox patrons at

Passengers wait in the 1700 block of Commonwealth Ave. to catch center-entrance car No. 6138 inbound for Lechmere via the subway. The year is 1933, and few are lucky enough to commute to work. *Boston Elevated Railway*

PCC car 3271 is bound for Boston College as it enters the present Haymarket Station on March 27, 1977, having just passed the platforms of the original Haymarket. The new station was built in the area formerly occupied by the tracks serving the Brattle Loop and was opened May 10, 1971. *Stephen P. Carlson*

nearby Fenway Park. This was an important junction, and the heavy ridership the company enjoyed here made this transfer station, later known as Kenmore Station, very important in short order.

On September 24, 1934, the Blandford St. cutback was started. It acted sometimes as a substitute and sometimes as an alternate cutback to Braves Field. Originally, it was just a crossover, but the third track installation at this location was added June 30, 1931. It remains in regular use today.

In 1922, the Boston Elevated made a proposal for the Allston-Brighton area which had important implications for the entire system as well. The company wanted to build a prepayment transfer station on Linden St., Allston, between Brighton and Commonwealth Aves. Cars coming from Lake St. and other parts of Allston and Brighton would discharge their passengers at this station. In a manner similar to the way the newly-opened Lechmere Station was handling riders, a transfer would be made to three-car center-entrance trains for downtown. Local opposition killed this plan, however, and Linden St. Transfer Station was never built.

In 1926, the Boston Elevated installed a passing siding near Washington St. and Commonwealth Ave., completing this work on October 27. This was periodically used over the years for cutbacks, and was removed on January 23, 1953.

A new lobby and yard were placed in service at Lake St. and Commonwealth Ave. September 12, 1930. The old waiting station in the center of Commonwealth Ave. was removed at this time, having served Auburndale and Boston riders for many years.

The Commonwealth Ave. line serves two of Boston's major educational institutions—Boston University just west of Kenmore Square and Boston College at the Chestnut Hill end of the line. In the late 1940s the destination LAKE ST. began to be replaced on car signs by the BOSTON COLLEGE indication by which the line is known today.

In the fall of 1953, Boston University, which had just purchased Braves Field from the departing team, informed the MTA of the University's intention to build athletic facilities on the site of the existing loop. The MTA wanted to retain the loop, but B.U. insisted that it needed the site. After fruitless negotiations, on January 15, 1962, the MTA finally did close the loop.

The Massachusetts Bay Transportation Authority opened a new maintenance facility for LRVs and an operator's lobby at Boston College May 23, 1979. The maintenance building was a "first" for this location.

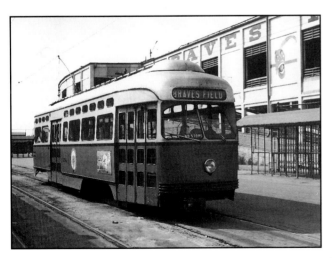

The 50 "Picture Window" PCC cars purchased in 1951 were the last new streetcars acquired for a quarter of a century. Newly delivered car 3292 sits at the Braves Field Loop. With the departure of the Braves for Milwaukee following the 1952 season, the stadium was sold to Boston University, leading to a lengthy debate between the MTA and B.U. over the future of this turnback facility. *Norton D. Clark, Carlson Collection*

E-*Arborway*
The Arborway Line

THE ARBORWAY LINE still officially runs from the Arborway at Forest Hills to Lechmere, but is presently operated only as far as Heath St. Loop. It has had a long and complex history. The first track on this line was laid in 1857, but the route we know today as E-*Arborway*, which leaves Forest Hills and follows South St., Centre St., South Huntington Ave., and Huntington Ave., finally entering the subway at Northeastern University, was not actually a through route until 1915.

The outer end of this line was the first segment to be built. In 1856, the West Roxbury Railroad obtained a horsecar franchise from the City of Roxbury and the Town of West Roxbury. In 1857, the company built a line from South and McBride Sts., West Roxbury, to Roxbury Crossing via South St., Centre St., Columbus Ave., and Tremont St., in the process running through the heart of Jamaica Plain. In 1857, the Metropolitan Railroad leased the West Roxbury Railroad. The Metropolitan immediately extended its tracks on Tremont St., Boston, to connect with the former West Roxbury Railroad trackage at Roxbury Crossing.

The new horsecar line was 4½ miles long, running from Tremont House in downtown Boston to Jamaica Plain Center. The fare was 10 cents and the trip by horse car took more than an hour. In 1858, the original rails of the West Roxbury Railroad were relaid because heavy ridership greatly exceeded the levels that the road had been built to handle. In addition, the Metropolitan double-tracked the Tremont St. section and part of Centre St. as far as Perkins St. to accommodate demands for more service. Also during 1858, the Metropolitan built along Centre St. from Columbus Ave. to John Eliot Sq. in

Track work on Huntington Ave. slowed open car 3210 down near the Museum of Fine Arts as it made its way to Park Street Station. The car was coming from Brookline rather than Jamaica Plain. Cars from the latter point would not use this trackage until 1903. *Boston Elevated Railway*

Roxbury. This line connected the Jamaica Plain trackage to the Metropolitan's first line on Washington St., giving Jamaica Plain residents two different routes to downtown Boston.

The next segment of E-*Arborway* was the section on Huntington Ave. between Tremont St., at Brigham Circle, and South Huntington Ave. This segment was part of a new single-track horsecar line, the permit for which had been granted to the Metropolitan Railroad by the City of Roxbury on August

Before the Huntington Avenue Subway opened, Boylston St. between Copley Square and Arlington St. was a very busy place. The Huntington Ave. car line was always very heavy; putting it underground speeded it and the street traffic which remained above considerably. *Boston Elevated Railway*

1, 1859, and which ran from Roxbury and Tremont Sts. along Tremont St. all the way to the Roxbury-Brookline boundary near Brookline Village. At that time, this section of Huntington Ave. was known as Tremont St.; it was not until January 5, 1895, that this segment was renamed Huntington Ave. The company was permitted to double-track this line on September 9, 1879.

The downtown section of the E-Line through Back Bay, which now runs through the Huntington Avenue and Boylston Street Subways, was constructed in the early 1880s. The City of Boston granted the Metropolitan Railroad the right on March 14, 1881, to build a double-track horsecar line on Huntington Ave. from Boylston St. at Copley Square to West Chester Park (now Massachusetts Ave.). On October 29, 1883, the company was granted the right to extend the tracks on Huntington Ave. from West Chester Park to Brigham Circle at Tremont St., joining the tracks on the outer end of Huntington Ave. which ran to Brookline Village, and which, as previously mentioned, had been in place since 1859.

In 1893, the tracks on Huntington Ave. were rebuilt and equipped for electric trolley car operation. On August 4, 1894, the West End Street Railway began running trolleys from Park and Washington Sts. in Brookline to Tremont House in downtown Boston via Brookline Village and Huntington Ave. Earlier, on October 14, 1891, the route from Jamaica Plain to the Northern Depots was electrified, including the tracks on South and Centre Sts. in Jamaica Plain.

After the Tremont Street Subway opened in September 1897, every section of the city wanted a direct connection to the subway. Jamaica Plain's turn came on November 1, 1898, when a line from Forest Hills to Park Street Station via Roxbury Crossing and Huntington Ave. was established. This route followed Washington St., Guild Row, Roxbury St., Shawmut Ave., Northampton St., Columbus Ave., Massachusetts Ave. and Huntington Ave. to Boylston St. and the subway.

The E-Line as we know it finally took shape in 1902 and 1903. On May 17, 1902, new tracks from Forest Hills to Jamaica Plain Carhouse on South St. were put into service. These tracks ran on South St. and on a short stretch of the Arborway. The missing link on South Huntington Ave. from Centre St. to Huntington Ave. was opened on July 11, 1903, and trolley

Type 4 No. 5358 has closed its doors at the Brigham Circle stop and is on its way to Heath Street Loop. Francis St. (Brigham Circle) was formerly a cutback point for this busy line, but it was moved to the new loop early in 1946. *Boston Elevated Railway*

tracks now ran directly from Forest Hills to Park Street Subway Station via the present-day E-Line route. To get to the subway by this route, however, a patron had to board a Columbus Ave. car at Forest Hills and take it to Jamaica Plain Carhouse on South St. From there the rider could board another car for the subway. This change of cars was not eliminated until 1915, when a true through route was finally established.

The major event in E-Line transit development was the opening of the Huntington Avenue Subway on February 16, 1941. This eliminated nearly a mile of extremely congested surface streetcar operation to Copley Square and took the last streetcars out of Copley Square itself. Service to Jamaica Plain was speeded up by more than 15 minutes by this improvement, and ridership on the line increased considerably.

The Francis St. (Brigham Circle)–Park Street Station cutback began on October 20, 1926. It ran until June 27, 1932, was temporarily discontinued, and then returned on June 25, 1934. On December 15, 1945, Heath St. Loop was opened. A new line running from Heath St. to North Station was established on January 3, 1946, replacing the Francis St.–Park Street Station service. The Heath St.–North Station service was discontinued on September 8, 1961, but by 1965, heavy ridership on the Huntington line had forced its resumption. The use of the crossover trackage at Brigham Circle has continued sporadically over the years for regularly-scheduled cutbacks and as a temporary terminal point.

PCC 3064 rolls down South Huntington Ave. past Bynner St. in this 1972 view. The Arborway line was the last subway service to utilize PCC cars. *Bradley H. Clarke*

Starting in January 1977, a shortage of streetcars forced the MBTA to cut back Arborway service to Heath St. In March 1977 full service was resumed to the Arborway. Again in October 1977 service was cut back to Heath St., but only on weekdays. Service over the next year to Arborway was resumed in part, but only at certain times. Finally, on September 7, 1979, Arborway service was completely restored.

Again, beginning on March 22, 1980, Arborway car service was interrupted—this time for more than two years because of surface and subway construction activity. Buses from Arborway to Copley Station replaced the through streetcar service, but an LRV shuttle was started from North Station to Symphony Station, to provide service in the Huntington Avenue Subway. On June 14, 1980, this shuttle was extended from Symphony to Northeastern University. On September 20, 1980, car service resumed from Northeastern to Brigham Circle. At last, on June 26, 1982, streetcar service resumed over the entire Arborway line. Again, however, from October 15 to November 11, 1983, the Arborway line closed for the relocation of tracks at Forest Hills to accommodate the Southwest Corridor Extension. Service interruptions on this line had continued for several years, resulting in full and off-peak period busing and an inconvenient transfer at Copley Station.

Finally, on December 28, 1985, the Arborway car line was closed for an indefinite period. It was replaced with bus routes 39 and 39H. The last streetcar trip from Arborway departed at 12:14 a.m. A two-car train was used, led by No. 3285 operated by Philip Robertson and followed by trailer No. 3261 with Richard Iddings as conductor. The train, with a large number of well-wishers aboard, left Park Street at 12:58 a.m., and it arrived back at Arborway at 1:27 a.m. The reason given for this change was road reconstruction work on Huntington Ave. This was the last revenue use of PCC cars in the subway. The subway between Copley and Northeastern was also temporarily closed at this time.

In 1988 LRV 3520 is about to enter the Northeastern stop on its way to Brigham Circle. From 1986 to 1989 Brigham Circle was the temporary terminus of the E-Line. *Bradley H. Clarke*

On July 26, 1986, LRVs began running as far as Brigham Circle, following track work in the Huntington Avenue Subway. Service was resumed to Heath St. on November 4, 1989, after track replacement on Huntington Ave. from Brigham Circle to South Huntington Ave. Today, streetcars on the E-Line run only to Heath St. Loop, while discussions about the future of streetcar service to Forest Hills continue between the community served by the line and the MBTA.

D-*Riverside*
The Riverside Line

PROPOSALS TO CONVERT THE HIGHLAND BRANCH of the Boston & Albany Railroad, a New York Central subsidiary, to a rapid-transit line had been made by the Massachusetts Division of Metropolitan Planning as early as 1926. On June 20, 1957, the General Court authorized the MTA to construct a rapid transit line from the Boylston Street Subway extension under Beacon St. over the Newton Highlands Branch of the Boston & Albany Railroad to a point in Newton westerly of Grove St. This required the approval of the MTA Advisory Board, the Department of Public Utilities, and the Interstate Commerce Commission for the railroad to abandon the branch. The Advisory Board approved the extension on October 1, 1957, and the Department of Public Utilities did so on December 6, 1957. The ICC followed with a certificate of abandonment early in 1958. The last trains ran on May 31, 1958, and on June 9, the MTA executed a construction contract for the project, not to exceed $9,200,000. The line was funded by a bond issue authorized by the Legislature.

The segment of the railroad branch to be used by the rapid transit line was 9.4 miles, and the total length of the run to Park Street was approximately 12 miles, which at that time was the furthest distance of any rapid transit line from downtown Boston. Major work included the construction of an 1,150-foot subway and incline; extensive connecting trackwork, a loop, a busway, passenger shelters, and storage space for streetcars at Reservoir Yard; a car storage yard and loop and a station at Riverside; and a new automatic substation for the line at the South Boston Power Station. Parking facilities were furnished at a number of stations. The largest lot was located at Riverside, holding 2,200 cars. Block signals were the same type as those used elsewhere in the Boylston and Tremont Street subway system. PCC streetcars from the existing fleet, running in three-car trains, would be used on the line.

The groundbreaking took place on July 10, 1958. The work was 41 per cent complete by December 31, 1958, with a target opening date of July 1, 1959. On June 11, 1959, the first streetcar test trip on the Riverside line occurred, with PCC cars Nos. 3090, 3091, and 3095 making a trip from Kenmore to Riverside and return. This was followed on June 30, 1959, by official inspection trips using three-car PCC trains. At Riverside, ceremonies and a luncheon took place, and Governor Foster Furcolo delivered the dedication of the Highland Branch Extension of the MTA at this time. The route has since be-

On Christmas Day 1974 PCC 3236 fights the snow as it loads passengers at the Brookline Village stop. The rapid transit shelter was quite different in character from the railroad station that preceded it. *Ginny Wisecup Crouse*

come known to all as the Riverside Line.

Revenue operation began on July 4, 1959. The first train consisted of cars 3295, 3311, and 3290, which left Riverside for Park Street at 6:50 a.m. The line was a runaway success, carrying 26,000 daily riders during the work week. The Boston & Albany Railroad had carried 3,140 riders daily in the same time period. Now the MTA carried as many riders during a peak hour as the railroad did in an entire day!

Late in June 1960, work began on expanding car storage and constructing a servicing facility at Riverside Yard. This work was completed January 12, 1961.

From September 7 to December 28, 1973, the Riverside line from Newton Highlands to Riverside was shut down for reconstruction. Outbound cars used a temporary loop at Cook St., west of Newton Highlands, until the work was completed. The section between Reservoir and Kenmore was then rebuilt between June 8 and September 11, 1974. During this period, Riverside cars diverted from this section to the Beacon St. line, using a temporary loop constructed in the Reservoir up-

In anticipation of the arrival of new cars, the Riverside line underwent extensive rebuilding in the early 1970s. The final section to be done was the segment between Cook Junction and Reservoir, where this July 1975 scene (above) was taken. *Chuck Crouse*

The new LRVs cut their teeth in Boston's tough winter weather, as this shot taken at Newton Highlands on February 2, 1977, demonstrates. *Norton D. Clark*

If the West End Street Railway failed to have a formal opening for the subway, its successors have honored major anniversaries. Here the principal kiosk at Park Street Station is decorated for the Diamond Jubilee celebration of September 1, 1972. On the left side of the kiosk is the plaque designating the Tremont Street Subway as a National Historic Landmark. *Daniel R. Cohen*

per yard. Reconstruction of the last segment between Reservoir and Cook Junction began in mid-September 1974 and continued through mid-November. Work resumed in the spring of 1975, finally winding up in November. During the construction periods, buses maintained service along the affected sections as required.

To maintain the new LRV fleet, a $10.1 million light rail vehicle maintenance facility was dedicated at Riverside on July 12, 1976. A new prepayment passenger terminal at Riverside has been under construction in recent years, but it is not yet open to the public.

Riverside is a true light rail line. It is an early and bold example of light rail technology in the face of the prevailing opinion of the 1950s which regarded streetcars as passé. Today, there is a resurgence of interest across the land in light rail. The Tremont Street Subway and its branches, now the Green Line, led the way and continue to, as they enter a second century of service to the people of Metropolitan Boston.

This Switchman's badge from the 1890s was typical of the metal badges of the period. This one was probably stamped out in the West End's shops. Note the soldered numbers askew. *Clarke Collection; photograph by J. David Bohl*

Recommended Reading

Bobrick, Benson. *Labyrinths of Iron: A History of the World's Subways.* New York: Newsweek Books, 1981.

Boston Elevated Railway Company. *Fifty Years of Unified Transportation in Metropolitan Boston.* Boston: Boston Elevated Railway Company, 1938.

Boston Transit Commission. *Annual Reports.* 1st (1894/95)-24th (1917/18). Boston: Boston Transit Commission, 1895-1918.

Carlson, Stephen P. *From Boston to the Berkshires: A Pictorial Review of Electric Transportation in Massachusetts.* Boston: Boston Street Railway Association, 1990.

Chiasson, George, Jr. *Boston's Main Line El: The Formative Years, 1879-1908.* New York: Electric Railroaders Association, 1995.

Clarke, Bradley H. *The Boston Rapid Transit Album.* Boston: Boston Street Railway Association, 1982.

Clarke, Bradley H. *The Boston Transit Album.* Boston: Boston Street Railway Association, 1977.

Cudahy, Brian J. *Cash, Tokens, and Transfers: A History of Urban Mass Transit in North America.* New York: Fordham University Press, 1990.

Cudahy, Brian J. *Change at Park Street Under: The Story of Boston's Subways.* Brattleboro, Vt.: The Stephen Green Press, 1972.

Cheape, Charles W. *Moving the Masses, A Study of Three Cities.* Cambridge: Harvard University Press, 1980.

Cummings, O. R. *Street Cars of Boston.* Vol. 1-6. Forty-Fort, Pa.: Harold E. Cox, 1973-1980.

Dana, Edward. *Riverside Line Extension, 1959.* Warehouse Point, Ct.: Connecticut Valley Chapter, National Railway Historical Society, 1961.

Miller, John Anderson. *Fares, Please!* 2nd ed. New York: Dover Publications, 1961.

Rapid Transit Commission. *Report of the Rapid Transit Commission to the Massachusetts Legislature, April 15, 1892.* Boston, 1892.

Schantz, James D., ed. *Budapest's Földalatti Subway and the Seashore Trolley Museum.* Kennebunkport, Me.: New England Electric Railway Historical Society, 1992.

About the Authors

BRADLEY H. CLARKE has had a life-long interest in mass transportation, particularly in electric railways. He has a bachelor's degree in Chemical Engineering from Northeastern University and is a project manager for Herzog-Hart Corp., a Boston architectural and engineering firm. This is Clarke's eighth book on public transportation in Massachusetts, and more are planned. He is president of the Boston Street Railway Association and a former trustee of the Seashore Trolley Museum. Clarke has lived in Massachusetts all his life. He grew up near Boston and now lives in the city.

O. R. CUMMINGS, also known to many as Dick Cummings, is a native of Newburyport, Mass., and moved to Manchester, N.H., in 1956. He was a reporter for the *Newburyport Daily News* from 1948 to 1956, and a rewrite man and copy editor for the *Manchester Union Leader* from 1956 until his retirement in 1987. He became an active trolley hobbyist in 1940 and wrote his first street railway history in 1948. Since then he has published more than 50 additional books about trolley lines in Maine, New Hampshire, and Massachusetts, and is working on histories of trolley freight and express operation in the Bay State and in Maine. His most ambitious effort was a six-volume series on the surface passenger cars purchased or built by the West End Street Railway and the Boston Elevated Railway.